for my very dear friends
Roy + Ann
with much love, Wendy

WALKING THE
BRITTANY COAST

VOL 2:
MORLAIX TO BENODET

GW00481962

Wendy Mewes

Walking the Brittany Coast
Vol 2: Morlaix to Benodet
published by Red Dog Books
ISBN 978 0 9557088 1 7

© text and photos Wendy Mewes 2008

The right of Wendy Mewes to be identified as the author of this
work is asserted in accordance with sections 77 and 78 of the
Copyright Designs and Patents Act 1988

British Library Cataloguing-in-Publication Data
A catalogue record for this book is available from the British Library

Red Dog Books is based in Axbridge, Somerset and in Brittany.
Enquiries should be addressed to the editorial office at
Red Dog Books, 29410 Plounéour-Ménez, France.

email: reddogbooks@orange.fr

www.reddogbooks.com

Printed and bound in China

For Rosemary Alexander
(1947-2008)

This book is dedicated to the memory of
my dear friend, who throughout her life
retained strong images of
the Breton coast from early sailing trips.

About the Author

Wendy Mewes has a Masters degree in ancient history and has worked on historical research for many years. Previous books include *Discovering the History of Brittany*, *Walking and other activities in Finistere*, and a guidebook to the Nantes-Brest canal. *The Five of Cups* is a novel based in the Monts d'Arrée, her home territory. She is also the President of the Brittany Walks Association, which promotes walking in Brittany to anglophones.

www.wendymewes.net

www.brittanywalks.com

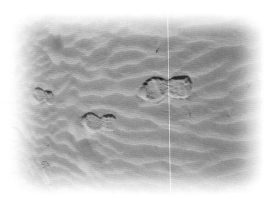

Acknowledgements

Warm thanks to friends who have helped with this book: in particular, Jeanne le Bourgeois for her company, Kay and Steve Attwell for testing my methods, and Les Keen for many lifts and lunches. Their encouragement and support have meant a lot.

Thanks also to all those in tourist offices (and other places) who provided information and expressed interest in the project. The Centre de documentation sur l'environnement in Quimper should be singled out for mention here.

CONTENTS

ABBREVIATIONS

CA	Continue ahead		D	Route Départementale (eg D10)
L	left			
R	right		GR	Grand Randonnée (long distance footpath)
TJ	T-junction			
P	parking		Mkt	market
km	kilometre		TO	Tourist Office
m	metres			

MAP SYMBOLS

⛪ abbey		⛯	lighthouse
✧ archaeological feature		〰	marsh
✳ belvedere		◊	menhir
(△/6) campsite		◉	mill
		△	monument
(1) chambres d'hôte		═	motorway
▲ chapel		Ⓜ	museum
✛ château		ℙ	parking
⛪ church		‖	path limit (see next/previous map)
† cross/calvaire		– – –	path to follow
⛩ dolmen		⋯⋯⋯	path alternative/detour
◪ electricity station		⋇	picnic area
≜ fontaine		▭▭▭	railway
☆ fort		(1)	rando-plume, rando-gîte
(❷) gîte d'étape		═══	road (surfaced)
⌂ hamlet		●	roundabout
(🏠) hotel		⊕	seamark
▲ houses		⨏	semaphore
▲ houses/town		═══	track
▫ lavoir		(3)	youth hostel

ABOUT THIS BOOK

The purpose of this guide is to give a detailed presentation of the Brittany coast, primarily for walkers, but also for all who enjoy fine scenery and interesting places, or simply want a sandy beach to lie on.

Most of the coast is accessible for walking, either by the GR34, a major footpath, other local paths or along beaches (depending on the tides) and dunes. A certain amount of road walking may be necessary in places, for ease of access or to avoid stretches of littoral impassable because of private property boundaries or unsafe cliffs. Some sections of the route suggested in this book may not be viable at the highest tides and road alternatives are usually suggested. Much of the time it is possible to ignore the directions altogether and just to walk along or behind the beach!

The introduction gives an overall view of the characteristics of coastal walking and a planning section at the end of the book covers factors to be taken into account when considering a walk along the littoral.

The glossary gives helpful terms of reference and vocabulary.

A list of abbreviations and map symbols used in the text is also included (opposite).

Each main chapter of the book deals with a section of coastline, working west from Morlaix, then down the Atlantic coast and finally eastwards to Benodet.

A brief introduction gives the overall length and flavour of the route, and highlights its attractions. Directions for walkers are then presented in full, using standard abbreviations (see p.6) in blue text.

The schematic scale maps mark the suggested route by a green broken line. Alternatives and diversions are shown by a dotted line. Each map is numbered and thus linked to the written directions. e.g. 24/3 in the directions refers to point 3 shown on map 24. Map symbols can be found on page 6.

Note on directions   The amount of detail in the directions does vary considerably, depending on the complexity of the route: towns and villages often require lengthier explanations than the concise presentation where the route is straightforward. Sometimes the route is obvious and the book is only necessary for back-up at those inevitable points where confusion sets in. Extra detail such as warnings, descriptive phrases and alternative routes are given in bold within the text of directions.

Information about sights along the way or within a short distance of the path is given in black in the text or in separate boxes. This is inevitably selective, and local tourist offices will be able to provide further suggestions for visits in each area.

At the end of each section, a box contains practical information about accommodation, services and transport. This list is not exhaustive, but a starting point for planning walking holidays. Consult the town websites given there for further information. Please note that we cannot guarantee the opening hours/months of shops, bars and restaurants or accommodation.

The places listed under services have at least basic shopping facilities (bakery and/or supermarket, and usually a cash-point) and refreshments in the form of a bar/café. Most have a range of eateries and shops. In the summer season many extra outlets will be open.

Note on Accommodation A selection of places on or very close to the coastal path is given, with the emphasis on B&B, camping and dormitory accommodation for walkers. This is only a small sample of what is available - the criteria of selection have generally been average prices and all year round opening. In the main, hotels are not listed, unless in special locations, nor B&B in towns – for these, consult the relevant tourist offices (details also given). Much accommodation is seasonal, so the choice will be greatest from June to September.

The transport details are designed primarily to help those planning linear walks, so taxi information and the website of local bus networks are given.

Suggestions for other walks in each area are given in brief. *Walking and other Activities in Finistere* and *Finistere:Things to see and do at the End of the World*, also by Wendy Mewes, are recommended for further reference.

The planning section at the end of the book has useful advice for preparing to walk the coastal path, with suggestions for the best walking if only a limited time is available.

An index of main place names is also included for ease of reference.

Colour photographs taken by the author are used throughout.

PLEASE READ

It is at all times the responsibility of each individual to decide on the advisability of a walk on the coast with regards to safety in respect of tides, high seas, and strong winds, especially on cliff paths.

Essential equipment should include proper footwear, bad weather protective clothing, an adequate supply of water and some form of communication device, whether a mobile phone or at the very least a whistle. Enjoy coastal walking, but please try to remain safety conscious.

INTRODUCTION

It has been a great pleasure to walk, or in many parts re-walk, the coast of Finistere for this book. Nowhere in Brittany, or indeed France, is there more dramatic scenery to be found, and the infinite variety of the littoral over these 619kms has to be experienced to be believed. Even the familiars of the coast – sea, rocks, beaches, dunes, cliffs, islands, boats and lighthouses – change in appearance with the weather, the seasons and the tides to provide a kaleidoscopic prospect for walkers.

Despite the attractions of lazing on a beach or sitting watching the endless interplay of sky and water, the coast is essentially a place of movement and activity – not just at the obvious level of sports like sailing, swimming, riding, surfing and sand-yachting, but also in the driving forces of natural elements which have shaped and reshaped the shore and hinterland over millions of years. And from the legendary arrival of Celtic saints in their stone boats to the only too real imposition of German U-boats during WWII, the Breton shores have also played a vivid role in the history of western Europe.

There is a very wide variety of terrain involved in coastal walking here, with something suitable for all levels of ability and stamina. For a short walk, level, well-made paths exist around some of the most spectacular viewpoints like the Pointe du Van and the Pointe du Raz. Many parts of the coast are relatively flat, and estuaries in particular, such as the Anse de Penfoul near Benodet, usually provide undemanding routes with good paths. Walking on sand can sometimes be surprisingly hard-going and, as many areas of environmentally sensitive sand-dunes are protected, there are often more solid footpaths to be found a little behind the coastline. The best beach walk is, without doubt, along the Baie d'Audierne.

Low headlands are common on the northern coast of Finistere with straightforward trails tracing a line of rocky coves, often past extraordinary rock formations and with excellent views to offshore islands and the memorable sight of Île Vierge, the tallest lighthouse in Europe. There are also many good swimming beaches in this area and for background a rare quality of light that intensifies shades of colour.

For an exceptional experience, however, the high cliffs of the Crozon peninsula or Cap Sizun have to be the jewel in the crown of coastal walking in Brittany. With many precipitous ups-and-downs and narrow,

uneven paths sometimes on the edge of significant sheer drops, these sections will test the knees and the head for heights of any walker. Having said that, the route is strenuous and challenging rather than off-puttingly hazardous: the most stunning sections of the coast are precisely those that require this amount of effort. Concentration is needed on these paths, but the rewards are great in terms of isolated splendour of views and atmosphere: a walk on the wild western coast from Kerloc'h to the Cap de la Chèvre is an unforgettable journey. To stand at the westernmost point of France at the Pointe du Corsen, north-west of Brest, also furnishes a most agreeable sensation, whether in sunshine or driving rain!

Walking the coast of Finistere will be an ecstatic experience for nature lovers. Bird-watchers can enjoy the sight of herons and egrets populating the numerous estuaries, marsh-dwellers of the étangs, spoonbills wintering in the Baie de Goulven and a host of seabirds at the Réserve de Goulien on Cap Sizun. I was lucky enough to see choughs on the cliff-top among the standing stones of Lagatjar on the Crozon peninsula. As for mammals, grey seals are resident in Breton waters round the island of Molène, and sightings of dolphins off the Atlantic coast are common.

There is a surprising variety of plants to be found along the shore, from heather and gorse dominating the heights and providing a blaze of colour for much of the year, to hardy marram grasses, thrift, samphire, sea-kale and a proliferation of orchids around the dunes. Seaweed spotting may seem an unusual activity, but Brittany lays claim to several hundred types, many visible around the rocks and beaches at low tide.

All these have their part to play in the intricate web of evolution of the littoral, and keeping to the paths helps to maintain the abundance and exuberance of the wildlife. The main environmental issues are conservation – dunes, marshes and other sea defences in particular - and the quality of water, not only for the tourist lure of good swimming but also for the growth of marine life. A major development in this context is the decision to establish the first national marine park in Brittany: the Parc naturel marin d'Iroise will cover a large section of the western coast of Finistere enabling much scientific study and the monitoring of coastal exploitation.

It is not only the natural glory of the land and seascape that provides a motivation for coastal walking. The edge of anywhere is always a place of potential tension and conflict, and the natural boundary of the sea makes no difference to this principle. There are many historical monuments and archaeological remains along the way, often only accessible on foot. Standing-stones (menhirs) and burial grounds positioned on the cliffs are a legacy from the new stone age when the Breton littoral was an important location of Neolithic settlement, whilst traces of occupation on rocky spurs protruding into the turbulent seas preserve the evidence of defensive systems from the Iron Age.

Help and guidance for those at sea has been provided in various ways over many centuries, from the fire towers of coastal abbeys such as that at St-Mathieu, west of Brest, to the semaphore stations and lighthouses that now line the coast. Climbing the 182 steps of the inland Phare de Trézien gives a magnificent view over the Mer d'Iroise towards the islands of Molène and Ouessant, and the handsome Kersanton stone Phare Eckmühl at Penmarc'h makes obvious the hazardous journeys facing sea-farers at the south-west tip of Brittany.

Religious buildings on the coast range from the grandiose ruined abbeys of St-Mathieu and Landévennec to marine chapels like St-They on the Pointe du Van or Notre-Dame de la Joie in St-Guénolé. The tiny chapel of St-Samson, on a lonely stretch of coast south of Trémazan, sticks in my memory as a fitting symbol of simple spirituality by the sea, in a position clearly chosen for its isolation.

Coastal defences in the form of forts, customs look-out posts and guard-houses are prolific, recalling the constant naval conflicts, mainly with the English navy, and the persistent endeavours of smugglers. A whole chain of forts master-minded by Vauban, Royal Engineer of Louis XIV, lines the shore on both sides of the approach to the Rade de Brest. Also much in evidence are the remains of structures, mostly lavishly graffitied these days, that formed the Atlantic Wall system of protection for the coast of Brittany during German occupation in WWII.

Evidence of sea-faring traditions and the economic exploitation of the coast are most clearly visible in ports such as Lanildut, centre of the seaweed industry, the harbour of Le Guilvinec, and Bloscon, the ferry terminal at Roscoff. Fishing is still an active occupation, with daily auctions as the catch comes in at many small harbours. There are interesting museums and centres of interpretation for subjects as diverse as seaweed (Lanildut, Plouguerneau), the coastal environment (Maison de la Baie d'Audierne), fishing (Haliotka at Le Guilvinec) and maritime history (Brest). On a more sombre note, the anchor of the Amoco Cadiz stands on the quay at Portsall, a reminder of the appalling pollution suffered by the Breton coasts for hundreds of kilometres as a result of that disaster.

Coastal walking certainly has its own particularities: there is nothing so satisfying as looking back on a long series of headlands (which can actually be covered in a surprisingly short time) and feeling a sense of great achievement. On the other hand, a more negative psychological aspect can be the many estuaries, which whilst providing some of the most attractive walking to be found in this book, also by their very nature have the most frustrating aspect of all – realising that there are many kilometres to go up to the head of the estuary and back again to reach a point only a couple of hundred metres away across the water!

The weather is often a factor in a good day's walk by the sea, but it is not always bright sunshine that is most welcome on a route that is largely exposed. Walking in sunshine with a light breeze to take the edge off the heat is certainly very pleasant, but to see this remarkable coast in all its moods, it is worth enduring a few rainy days or a winter walk – in fact, December is one of my favourite times for walking in Brittany.

Walking close to the sea is possible for much of the way but diversions are necessary where private property intrudes or the terrain and tides do not permit easy passage. I have tried to give road alternatives in many places, but often it is possible and even pleasurable to do a bit of rock-scrambling and remain near to the water. I would emphasise, however, that care is needed at all times with regard not only to what is underfoot, but also to the tides and weather in general.

Overall my essential memories of this very rewarding experience will be the sea breeze on my face – with resultant salty skin and hair day after day - the scent of pine and heather, sea shades ranging from black to the lightest turquoise, the weird and wonderful shape of rock formations, the cries of a hundred different birds, the slithering dart of lizards, the chug of fishing boats and the silent progress of a yacht in full sail across a gentle bay. It is also hard to forget the utter difference of scene wrought by the level of the tide, so that even a single spot seems to change its very nature according to the time of day and year.

Finally, if this book gives you a taste for the great variety and richness of the landscape in this special part of Brittany, details of many other walks and places to visit in Finistere can be found in my books *Walking and other Activities in Finistere* and *Finistere: Things to see and do at the End of the World*. Happy walking!

Wendy Mewes

1. MORLAIX to ROSCOFF
Baie de Morlaix
41 kms

Our journey starts in the exceptional town of Morlaix, which warrants exploration of the medieval centre and stepped passageways before continuing up the river estuary. A coast road runs alongside the water much of the way here but it is not a very safe or comfortable walk and so an inland diversion via the very attractive little bourg of Locquénolé is recommended.

Carantec with its beaches and fish restaurants has all the appeal of a typical seaside resort and further good bathing opportunities follow around St-Pol-de-Léon. If religious architecture appeals, the cathedral and famous chapel here are also worth a short diversion into the town. Islands are a theme of this section with the memorable sight of the Château de Taureau at the entrance to the estuary, the causeway crossing to Île Callot which is only accessible at low tide, and Îlot Ste-Anne, the perfect spot for a relaxing pause.

MORLAIX

The château on one of Morlaix's three hills has long since disappeared and the town today is dominated by a towering viaduct that carries the Brest-Paris railway. This was built in 1861-4, to a height of 60m, and shortened the journey time to the capital from 62 to 16 hours. During allied bombing in 1943 one arch was destroyed, as well as a school nearby, where a commemorative chapel now stands.

Historically the town is on the border of two episcopal districts, a fact reflected in the names of the Quai de Tréguier and Quai de Léon. Not exactly in the main stream of Breton history, it nevertheless saw action in the 14th century Wars of Succession and a siege during the religious Wars of the League. Morlaix also gave hospitality to important visitors such as Anne de Bretagne, who lodged in the Convent des Jacobins, as Mary Stuart (aged 6) did 43 years later, on her way to marry the Dauphin, later François II of France.

In 1522 Morlaix was sacked by the English whilst its soldiers and merchants were absent. The Comte de Laval led an avenging force which caught many stragglers who had lingered to drink to their success in the woods above the port. The Fontaine des Anglais on the Quai de Tréguier today is a reminder of when the stream ran red with English blood.

As a result of this experience, the Château de Taureau was built on an island in the Bay of Morlaix to protect the river mouth. Another possible legacy was the punning motto adopted by the town much later - S'ils te mordent, mords-les (If they bite you, bite them back).

The medieval heart of the city with its cobbled streets and half-timbered houses is just behind the imposing Hôtel de Ville. No 9 Grand Rue is now part of the town museum and provides an exceptional exhibition of a unique architectural form – la maison à pondalez, from pont + aller, a reference to the wooden 'bridges' to front and back rooms from a central turning stair with a space between spanning all four storeys. Many ancient stepped alleyways (venelles) riddle the hillsides around the centre providing alluringly different perspectives.

On Saturdays an excellent market fills the town centre, with fresh local produce in the Place Allende and varied stalls by the viaduct.

CHARLES CORNIC

Charles Cornic (1731-1809) was a famous corsair who achieved extraordinary exploits against the English. In 1752, for example, he managed to capture three ships, despite 120 cannon against his own 30. In the later part of his life, he made an equally valuable contribution to naval history by mapping the bay and estuary of Morlaix.

DIRECTIONS (see map on next page)

1/1 From viaduct, approach river via Place de Cornic • **CA**, past bust of Charles Cornic, keep river on **R**. **This is the former port area; the old tobacco factory is on your left** • At mini-roundabout go **L** uphill (past new Auberge de Jeunesse) • 200m turn **R** on footpath into wood • At top of steps go **R** • **CA** past lavoir on **L** after 100m and another on **R** soon after • Climbing, at fork in path, **EITHER** go **R** for little loop with views of river **OR** go straight on to cut this out • **CA** at fork soon after, then **ahead** at junction of four paths further on • At track, turn **R** (former railway) and follow 1.5kms over bridge, through **P** and under motorway • At end go down to road and bear **L** in front of *Maison de Retraite* • **The original 15th century convent here became an Augustine establishment in 1834. The ancient (1527) and tower-less church of St-François has a small museum of religious treasures and a cloister**

THE PORT

The heyday of Morlaix's international commerce was the 15th-18th centuries, when the river gave access to three-masted ships. Linen, tobacco, leather, paper and butter were exported to markets in England, Portugal, Spain, Holland and Hamburg. This was also a stage on the Bordeaux wine route. Ship building was another thriving industry – in 1500 the famous 700 tonnes Cordelière (see p.88) was constructed here by Nicolas de Coetanlem, commissioned by Anne de Bretagne.

The production of tobacco began in Morlaix in the 17th century at a nearby manoir and moved here to the quai de Leon in 1736. Up to 1000 people were employed at the height of its success, but the monopoly was lost after the French Revolution and production declined.

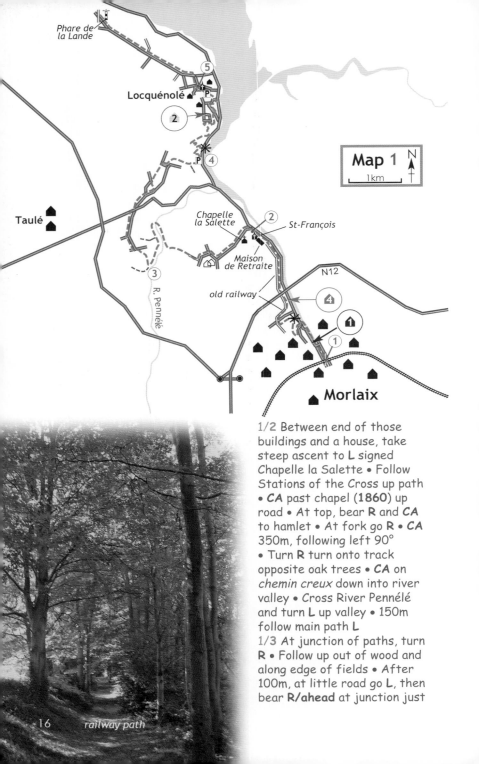

Phare de la Lande

Locquénolé

Taulé

Map 1 N
1km

Chapelle la Salette
St-François

Maison de Retraite

old railway

N12

R. Pennéié

Morlaix

1/2 Between end of those buildings and a house, take steep ascent to **L** signed Chapelle la Salette • Follow Stations of the Cross up path • **CA** past chapel (**1860**) up road • At top, bear **R** and **CA** to hamlet • At fork go **R** • **CA** 350m, following left 90° • Turn **R** turn onto track opposite oak trees • **CA** on *chemin creux* down into river valley • Cross River Pennélé and turn **L** up valley • 150m follow main path **L**
1/3 At junction of paths, turn **R** • Follow up out of wood and along edge of fields • After 100m, at little road go **L**, then bear **R/ahead** at junction just

after • At next junction, go **R** • Go **ahead** between huge glasshouses • At main road go **R** 50m then **L** • 300m, fork **R** • On left bend, take narrow footpath **L** • At road, go **R** then immediately **R** again on path across middle of fields • At next road, go **R** 100m then **L** on narrow footpath • Follow downhill into woodland, cross stream, then bear **R** downhill at junction of paths • At fork go **L** down to ℙ on main road

1/4 Turn **L** through ℙ, then **L** up into trees by wooden sign • At top of steps go **R** • At look-out point, follow path sharp **L** up hill, to double back high above estuary • Continue up broad path, ignoring others • At top, go **R** at **TJ** of paths • 300m where track divides turn **R** downhill • At bottom of steps, go **R** then **L** before exit to road • Continue up steps into wood again • Keep ahead uphill, ignoring other paths (Ignore **R** turn sign on tree) • Follow **L** then turn **R** towards road • Go **R** on road • 120m at left bend, go **R** down *chemin vert* • 30m turn **L** on footpath • Follow 350m, at end follow **R** to road • Turn **L** along road • 250m at **TJ** turn **R** downhill • Follow road round to left, then bear **R** immediately down to shore • At main road, bear **L** before playground • Follow past playground, through ℙ, towards Locquénolé church • **The name Locquénolé means 'sacred place of St-Guénolé (see p.111). The attractive 17th century church here retains elements of an earlier foundation.**

Chapelle la Salette

L'ARBRE DE LA LIBERTÉ
'Liberty' trees were planted all over France at the time of the Revolution. This one, the last surviving in Finistere, was planted on January 14th 1794, an occasion of celebration and dancing around the tree.

1/5 Keep church on right and go across paved area past L'Arbre de la Liberté • Bear **L** up path, bearing **R** to road at top • Cross over to follow road opposite (to **R** of cross) • **CA** to roundabout, bear **L** • **CA** on road 1.8km • Fork

Tree of Liberty

17

R to Phare de la Lande

2/1. Follow road past lighthouse
PHARE DE LA LANDE *Charles Cornic (see p.15) campaigned for a seamark on this site (and the Île Louët) after witnessing many shipwrecks in the estuary. The current lighthouse (19m) dates from 1845.*

• At end of road, **CA** on footpath
• Go **L** at road, follow to main road by water • Cross main road, go **ahead** on access road • Take path behind building, then follow by estuary то 🅿 • Through 🅿 towards beach, take path on **L** • Follow above beach 1km

2/2 Go ahead through 🅿, then bear **R**, keeping behind *viviers* buildings, through working area • **CA** to end of little road, then go **L** up steps
• At top go **ahead** up road • At mini-roundabout, go **R** 110m
ALTERNATIVES: EITHER (to cut out oyster farm) **CA** on road 600m, then ahead on footpath to sea-mark tower on point (**3**)
OR turn **R**, go down lane towards water, then ahead right through buildings • At end bear **R**, then keep behind buildings to continue along the coast • Go ahead across beach (made of oyster shells), along path by wall, then up steps and follow path through trees (**Views of Château de Taureau and Île Louët with lighthouse ahead**) to sea-mark tower on point (**3**)

2/3 From the marker, **CA** on path above beach (ignore steps down), keeping nearest to edge (Île Callot now visible ahead) • At three way split of paths, take middle one ahead • At a **TJ** go **R** to go out to point and back, **L** to continue • At 🅿, bear **R** and **CA** on path above beach (**This comes down to the main beach, sailing centre and restaurants**) • **CA** along beach, past embarkation point for Château du Taureau (see p. 19)

Île Louët

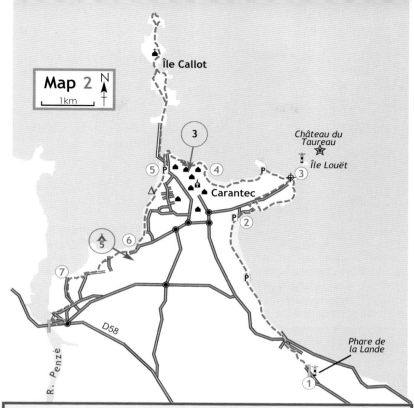

Map 2 — Île Callot, Île Louët, Château du Taureau, Carantec, Phare de la Lande, R. Penzé, D58

CHÂTEAU DU TAUREAU

This fort was built in 1544 to protect the Bay of Morlaix and river access to the town, and later restored by Vauban in his organisation of coastal defences (see p.86, 96). After 1721 it became a prison, catering mainly for deranged aristocrats consigned there by their families, although political prisoners were also held here, like La Chalotais (an opponent of the Governor of Brittany) in 1765 and Louis Auguste Blanqui, a socialist revolutionary, in 1871.

In the 20th century the château became the residence of Melanie Leveque de Vilmorin whose parties (and personal life) were famous. It was used by the Germans in WWII, before becoming a sailing school in the 1960s. Finally recognised for its historical value, the Château de Taureau was fully restored and opened to the public in 2006.

A visit to the Château by boat takes about 2 hours. In season, booking in advance is necessary. For this, see www.chateaudutaureau.com

19

At end of beach go up steps and bear **R** • At fork, bear **R** in front of seats • Keep above water on this path, ignoring those off to left (**Views of Île Callot, St-Pol and ferry at Roscoff**) • At road go **R**, follow round to **L** by water again • Cross top of beach 35m, then up steps – NOT first set, but through rocks, then around front wall of elaborate house, on concrete path • **CA** along next beach on sand • Go up slipway between walls, then ahead down steps behind wall, back to the beach • **CA** along beach (or through Ⓟ and along road) to come out on road that crosses causeway • Turn **R** here to visit Île Callot, otherwise **L** (**There is a noticeboard with tide times here – check before going to Île Callot**)

CARANTEC and ÎLE CALLOT

This is a very popular holiday destination, thanks to its excellent beaches, sailing facilities, coastal walks and the attraction of the causeway connection to Île Callot, which is cut off at high tide. This island was once a thriving centre of the fishing and seaweed industries. Now it is thronged in summer by visitors walking the 2km length to the table of orientation and the Chapelle de Notre-Dame de Callot near the end.

2/5 Go past Ⓟ and restaurants, and where road turns inland, go **R** along beach, passing Sibiril monument and carefully negotiating rails running into sea

(**ALTERNATIVE**: easier route by road as far as 2/6 - see map)

Causeway to Île Callot

Estuary of the Penzé from the Pont de la Corde

ERNEST SIBIRIL

By the shore there is a commemorative stele to resistance hero Ernest Sibiril. His family boat-building business was used as a cover to get 193 people safely across the channel in small black-painted craft under the noses of German surveillance on this highly defended coast. Eventually forced to escape himself, Sibiril reached England in Le Requin and joined the American navy as a pilot. He returned to Carantec after the war and General de Gaulle visited the shipyard in 1950 to pay tribute to his bravery and enterprise.

• **CA** 1.5kms • 150m after seamark (painted black and white) go through rocks onto road and turn **R**

2/6 **CA** to end of road, then **ahead** along edge of field • Keep ahead on broad path through middle of vegetable field • Cross little road and go **ahead** on track • **CA** on grassy path between banks, swinging inland • At **TJ** with track, go **R** • **CA** on road, bearing **L** uphill • 80m turn sharp **R** downhill on green path, bearing **L** behind buildings and along edge of field • Follow **L** between fields, then turn **R** at 90° towards estuary • Follow down to road

2/7 Go **L** on road 350m, then **R** at crossroads (before main road) • Fork **R** just after • At bottom go **L** • **Opposite is a stele commemorating Jacques Gueguen who smuggled members of the resistance and English soldiers out of France in his boat the Pourquoi-Pas. Denounced and arrested, he was imprisoned but survived the war** • 30m go **R** along track by water • At fork go **R** by edge of water, through working area • **CA** along beach towards bridge • Under bridge turn **L** up little road 250m to roundabout • Turn **R** and cross Pont de la Corde

3/1 Over bridge, bear **R** on little road • Follow to main road again, go **R**, then **R** again • Follow track 200m, then follow **L** to little road going inland • 150m go **R** on track • In hamlet go **R** and follow round to **L** past lavoir • At road go **R**, follow 1.2kms (**After 600m, up a track to the left, is a dolmen**) • At Keriven, at left bend, go **ahead** to **R** of lavoir, along edge of field • 80m, bear **L** across middle of field • Follow **R** 80m, then **L**, keep left of wood • 175m follow path **R**, down towards water, then up again to **L**

3/2 At road by house go **ahead** • At junction in hamlet go **ahead** (towards cross on hill) • 150m, at left bend, turn **R** beside house, up bank **ahead** on narrow footpath • At junction of paths by fence, go **R** downhill (To go up onto hill with cross go ahead along fence and bear left at the road – after a few paces, a path goes up **L** through the gorse) • At road go **L**, then

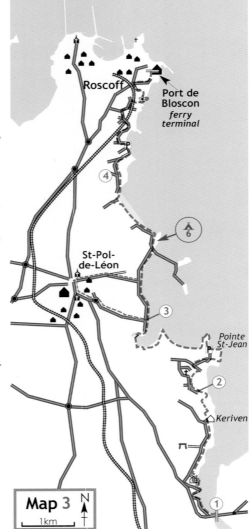

Roscoff

Port de Bloscon
ferry terminal

St-Pol-de-Léon

Pointe St-Jean

Keriven

Map 3
N
1km

dolmen

R • Follow 450m, then bear **R** (low wooden sign) through bank to follow path round headland, Pointe St-Jean (Alternative: stay on road to ⓟ to cut out Pointe St-Jean) • Go through ⓟ, then bear **R** on path above beach (**Views of the Kreisker tower in St-Pol**) • **CA** on path behind hedge, or walk along sand • Keep bearing **R** on this path to follow around headland (View of Îlot St-Anne) • **CA** above beach (Grève de Kervigou) • Cross beach access road, **CA** up steps (chapel in trees on left) • Follow round another point, then back around creek • Bear **R** along wall of château and across causeway • **CA** on road past old gatehouse

CHÂTEAU DE KERNEVEZ There was a medieval château on this site, but the current building dates from the mid-19th century, when a fine estate of parkland and farms was developed.

3/3 **DETOUR**: To visit St-Pol, turn **L** here, follow road 1km to roundabout. There go **L** to Kreisker Chapel (very tall spire). There turn **R** to reach the cathedral. To return to the coast, go **R** before the cathedral (rue 4 Août 1944) and **CA**, past another chapel. At entrance to park, either go through it up to orientation table beyond cross, or bear **R** on the road to get back to the coast quickly

MAIN ROUTE: **CA** by water • Go on road briefly through houses, then

ST-POL-DE-LEON

St Pol came from Wales in the 5th century and was given land on the nearby Île de Batz (see p.28) by a local lord. He freed the area from a marauding dragon by using his stole to lead it to the edge of the cliffs and a watery destruction. There is a statue recalling this legend in the current Cathedral St-Paul Aurelien here, where Pol became bishop in the earliest religious foundation.

It is the Chapelle du Kreisker, however, that catches the eye with its huge tower (78m) dominating the town skyline. In a dilapidated state after the French Revolution, it was saved from destruction by an order of Napoleon who agreed to restoration by an order of 1807 on the grounds that it was a useful aid to navigation!

Îlot Ste-Anne

along coast behind seawall • **CA** to end of beach

DETOUR: Turn **R** on road out to Îlot Ste-Anne (**There are excellent views from the huge rock at the end of this promontory, which also retains evidence of fortifications from the 16th century onwards.**)

• **CA** on road (Camping Ar Kleguer here and another 400m further on) • At long shingly beach of Kersaliou, **CA** along road (**View of ferry port at Roscoff ahead**) • Where road turns inland, go up steps on **R** along path behind hedge • Cross little bridge, then open grassy area, before turning inland • At road go **R** towards water • Turn **L** along beach 40m, then up road past sitting area, bearing **R** along it

3/4 At left bend, bear **R** along Chemin de Kerfissiec • At fork, bear **R** downhill to water • Follow through P then take little road to **L** at very end of P • 150m turn **R** between houses on narrow road • Follow beside railway, then downhill and round to left • Over bridge, go **R** at junction • 150m at junction go **R** again • Bear **L** before railway bridge • Continue alongside railway 150m, then **R** under bridge • Pass entrance to exotic gardens on left, bear **R** to continue on coast path

• Go **L** at picnic area, following boundary of exotic garden • 100m after path turns inland along fence, go **R** at fork of paths • Another 100m, go **L** on grassy track • 80m to TJ, go **R** alongside railway • At main road go **R**, then immediately **R** again to walk down to ferry port • Cross P to main terminal, go to **L** of it to pick up path again

LE JARDIN EXOTIQUE

This garden of sub-tropical and exotic plants has over 3000 specimens and a spectacular rocky look-out point over the bay. Outside the winter months, it is open for part of most days.

1. PRACTICAL INFORMATION

SHOPS & SERVICES
- **Morlaix** TO open all year 02 98 62 14 94 www.morlaixtourisme.fr
  Mkt Sat
- **Carantec** TO open all year 02 98 67 00 43 www.ville-carantec.com
  Mkt Thurs
- **St-Pol-de-Léon** TO 02 98 69 05 69 www.saintpoldeleon.fr Mkt Tue
- **Roscoff** TO 02 98 61 12 13 www.roscoff-tourisme.com Mkt Wed

ACCOMMODATION
Hotels
1. Hôtel du Port (on route) Quai de Léon, 29600 Morlaix 02 98 88 07 54
   www.lhotelduport.com

Chambres d'hôte
2. Mme Pailler (200m) 23 Rubalan, 29670 Locquénolé 02 98 72 24 83
   jaouenpailler@yahoo.fr
3. Ti' Case (300m) Danielle Mugnier, 9 rue Maréchal Foch,
   29660 Carantec 06 62 13 60 67 www.chambre-ticase.com

Gîte d'étape
4. Le Logis des Ecluses (500m) 28 allée Saint-François, 29600 Saint-
   Martin-des-Champs 02 98 62 66 80 www.lelogisdesecluses.com

Camping
5. Village les Mouettes (150m) 29660 Carantec 02 98 67 02 46
   www.les-mouettes.com May-Sept.
6. Camping Ar Kleguer (on route) Plage Ste-Anne, 29250 St-Pol-de-Leon
   02 98 69 18 81 www.camping-ar-kleguer.com April-Sept

TRANSPORT
Train services: Morlaix station (02 98 15 20 05) on Paris/Brest main line.
Branch line to Roscoff (30 mins) www.sncf.com

Bus services: Morlaix/Roscoff www.viaoo29.fr

Taxi: Guy Laviec 02 98 88 35 43 Morlaix
Laurent Le Pors 02 98 67 00 00 Roscoff

Boat to Château de Taureau from Carantec: booking 02 98 62 29 73
www.chateaudutaureau.com

Ferry port at Roscoff (Bloscon) – Brittany Ferries to Plymouth or Cork

Ferry to Île de Batz from Roscoff harbour – various times daily

OTHER WALKS

For a town walk around the stepped
passageways and medieval centre of
Morlaix, see *Walking and other
Activities in Finistere*.

A 10km circuit of the Île de Batz
explores all sections of the island.

2. Roscoff - Plouescat
Haut Léon
38 kms

The town of Roscoff has very much more to offer than a ferry terminal: many ancient buildings and an atmospheric port area retain the image of its maritime past. It takes a long time to shake off the less attractive built-up environs, but once out on the coast towards Dossen things open up, and marine views include the Île de Batz and the Île de Siec just offshore. A taste of the large, curious granite rock formations typical of this northern coast is good preparation for the spectacular sights to come. The peaceful Anse of Guillec brings the variety of estuary scenery with its characteristic combination of sandy beaches and marshy beds, before the route returns to the sea with a long stretch of largely unspoilt littoral. There are good swimming opportunities in the many bays along this relatively flat stretch of coast, and the terrain provides easy, mostly level walking. For lovers of ancient history, Theven is an interesting Bronze/Iron age archaeological site, and two Neolithic monuments, a menhir and an unusual burial place, enliven the end of this section.

ROSCOFF

As early as the 15th century, ships from the port of Roscoff were active all over Europe. A major route to Spain saw the transport of grain and cloth in exchange for cargoes of olive oil and wine. By 1700, ships were travelling as far afield as Riga and Newfoundland. War and trade rivalries with England and Holland stimulated vigorous activity here as a base for corsairs who were given official permission to 'course' the enemy, destroying ships and seizing goods. In the late 18th century smuggling became a major occupation, when tea and wine attracted high customs duties for entering English ports.

The plain of Leon has long been a prime vegetable growing area – artichokes, onions, cauliflowers and carrots in particular – and these were shipped to Paris from Roscoff in the days before the railway network was developed. In 1828 the famous onion trade with England began when a farmer and his companions took a boatload of local oignons rosés across the Channel. This led to the phenomenon of the Johnnies, itinerant onion-sellers who travelled as far as Scotland with their wares. A museum in Roscoff celebrates their history and a festival in their honour is held here each August.

Roscoff had the first thalassotherapy centre in France at the end of 19th century after work by Dr Louis Bagot, and became renowned for the efficacy of its seawater-based treatments, which are still popular here today. There is also a Centre de Découverte des Algues for discovering the many varieties and usages of seaweed.

Practical developments at the port saw the erection of a 527m pier (1969) – looking like a footbridge to nowhere - to allow ferries to the nearby Île de Batz to operate at all tides, and the following year a deep water harbour was begun at Bloscon. This is now the home of Brittany Ferries, founded in 1972 by Alexis Gourvennec as an agricultural initiative, with ships taking produce to Plymouth for markets in Cornwall. Passenger trade and an extension of routes to Ireland and Spain developed later.

ÎLE DE BATZ

A 10 minute boat ride from Roscoff, the Île de Batz is a perfect rest day venue. Walking right round will only take 3-4 hours and the route includes the legendary scene of St-Pol's famous triumph over a marauding dragon (symbol of paganism) at Toull ar Zarpant (serpent) on the western coast (see p. 23).

Also well worth a visit are the exotic gardens established in the 19th century by Georges Delaselle, with a collection of more than 1,700 species of plants from the five continents. For superb views, the lighthouse is open mid-June to mid-September.

DIRECTIONS (see map on next page)

4/1 Facing the ferry terminal, follow white GR34 sign on **L** • At top of small Ⓟ go through wooden barrier onto coast path • At tarmac area, bear **L** across road, then ahead up to Chapelle St-Barbe • From chapel, cross Ⓟ, turn **R** on road passing beach • 200m go **R** - rue de Capitaine Coadou (no through road) • At grassy play area follow sea-front to far end of port area/Centre Nautique • Turn **L** inland • **The arched doorway on the left is all that remains of the chapel where the young Mary Queen of Scots gave thanks for surviving a stormy crossing in 1548**

CHAPELLE STE-BARBE

Perched on a conical hill this early 17th century chapel acted as a landmark for sailors and a focus for prayers for protection at sea. The Johnnies travelling to England to sell their onions hoisted their sails three times in passing to honour the saint.

From the observation point by the chapel there is a good view of the Île de Batz and, below, the Viviers de Roscoff where shellfish are bred, with the Pointe de Bloscon beyond. This defensive position was briefly occupied by the English in the mid-14th century during the Wars of Succession to the Dukedom of Brittany. In 1694 it was refortified with a drawbridge and cannon emplacements.

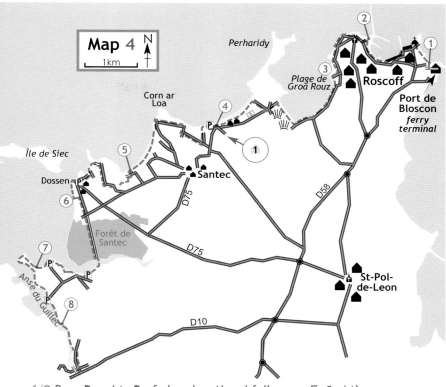

4/2 Bear **R** and to **R** of church • Ahead follow rue E. Corbière • Immediately bear **R** (signed 'Station Biologique') to sea front, bear **L** along boulevard • At end bear **R** onto road, Ave. Victor Hugo • **CA** on rue Marquise de Kergariou • Turn **R** into Allée de Groa Rouz, follow to coast at Plage de Groa Rouz

4/3 Follow path above beach • Rejoin road on bend and **CA** 1100m • Turn **R** (balisage) • Follow causeway between marsh and bay • At end, turn **L** along road • Cross next road and bear **R** following Circuit Perharidy sign • Continue up tarmac road with P and high hedges either side • At end turn **L** on narrow sandy path above beach • Follow between houses and beach

4/4 At café/bar go ahead into ⓟ

Here a plaque commemorates the Canadian destroyer HMCS Athabaskan, torpedoed by a German E-boat on 29 April 1944, with the loss of 128 lives. Victims were buried in eight cemeteries in Finistere, most at Plouescat. One of the survivors, Stuart Kettle, became a prisoner of war and kept a log of his experiences, which includes a poem about the fatal day:

"Some wanted to give up the fight
To sleep for evermore,
We did our best to give them strength
Till we hit the distant shore"

• Through gap in hedge at end of ⓟ, **CA** above sandy beach • Bear **L** through wooden barrier to road • follow to **TJ** and turn **R** • 500m to another **TJ**, turn **R** • Turn **L** on road just before beach • At end, turn **L** to continue along coast

DETOUR: turn **R** (balisage) for circuit of 800m to panoramic view at Corn ar Loa

• Walk along beach 1.1kms • 100m before end, turn **L** up access road

4/5 30m at **L** bend, turn **R** onto left-hand of two tracks • Follow **L** then **R** over fields • At cross-path, go **L**, then **R**, to right of houses towards road • Turn **R** on road • At end turn **L** on track • Behind point with big rock formation (pictured left), go **L** on shady path above rocky beach • At road **CA** 100m to take narrow path on **R** between concrete fences • Cross ⓟ then follow road to tarmac ⓟ overlooking bay. This is Dossen, where there are toilets, restaurants and bars • Continue along coast path behind lifeguards' hut

The **île de Siec** with its lone farm is visible across the water. This was once the centre of a thriving sardine fishing operation. The island was also the location of a defensive battery from the 18th century to WWII.

A memorial stone recalls the *Catastrophe de Dossen* in September 1944 when, during the clearing of mines, a cartload of them exploded and caused much death and damage.

4/6 300m turn **inland** at grassy area, take left-hand path through to road • Turn **R** and follow road 500m • At left bend, go **ahead** through  P • Continue on track through *Forêt Dominale de Santec* **(a parcours sportif runs alongside)** • At wide estuary **(with reedy marsh and good stretches of sand when the tide is low)** turn **L** then **R** over old slab bridge • On other side turn **R** along coast • Ahead through P continue to road, turn **R** • 50m round corner bear **R** off road and cross grassy area to coast path • 600m go through P, and through wooden barrier at far end onto another path

4/7 At fork in path, bear **R** to go round Pointe de Theven (for short-cut go **L** at junction of paths with big wooden signs) • At fork in path bear **L** inland to P • From P exit, turn **R** down road then **L** onto narrow coast path along edge of farming land

---

THEVEN PEN AR DOUR

This site was occupied as early as the Mesolithic era (c10,000BC) by hunter-gatherers, when the sea was at least 10m lower. It was an important burial place in the Bronze Age, with many finds preserved in the sandy soil. Traces of Iron Age cultivation and field boundaries have also been identified. An information board has a plan of the site.

4/8 At junction turn **R** down steps • CA on narrow path along estuary • Up steps, through barrier, to road, turn **R (Camping Bois de Palud up steps opposite)** • 400m at stone bridge, turn **R**

5/1 Follow road **R**, then on second bend take narrow path on **R** • At road follow **R**, between Moulin de Kerlan and Manoir on **L** • At P turn **R** along edge of field • Follow round edge of fields, with estuary below **(Views across to Sibiril church on left)**

5/2 Cross over little road to go up steps ahead (wooden board marked)

MANOIR DE KERLAN

Visible from the road, this 15/16th century manoir was built in the traditional style with a stair turret and closed courtyard. It was the headquarters of Leaguers besieging the nearby Château of Kerouzéré during the Wars of Religion at the end of the 16th century. The mill of the same name, built of blocks of granite on the bank of the Guillec, was mentioned by the writer Flaubert on his travels in Léon. It ceased operation in 1905, when the wheel was taken down.

• Follow uphill away from estuary, through wooden barrier and up steps • Descend into woods, emerging to skirt another huge field. **It is easy to see the essential character of the Leon landscape here: this is a major vegetable-growing area** • Down steps, across track and up more steps (or right to cove) • Narrow winding path through hedges, then along another field • Bear **R** onto gravel track • 30m bear **R** along narrow path; through wooden barriers soon after • **CA** along another field • Come out before little bay of Moguériec and round last field • Follow path between hedges again (huge boulders in garden on left) • Go through barrier, turn **R** (not down steps to rocks) and immediately **L** • **Tantalisingly close view of harbour but there's another inlet to go round first** • **CA** through working area of port (sign by entrance warns walkers enter at their own risk) to go round estuary

5/3 Before road, turn **R** behind bush on little path up wooden steps • Along edge of field, then bear **R** through barrier • **CA** on earth path • At road, go ahead bearing **R** • Bear **R** again at junction • At junction opposite bar/hotel, turn **L** up road • 350m turn **R** between two houses

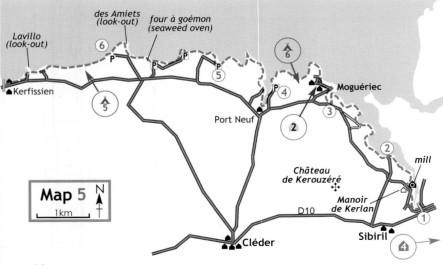

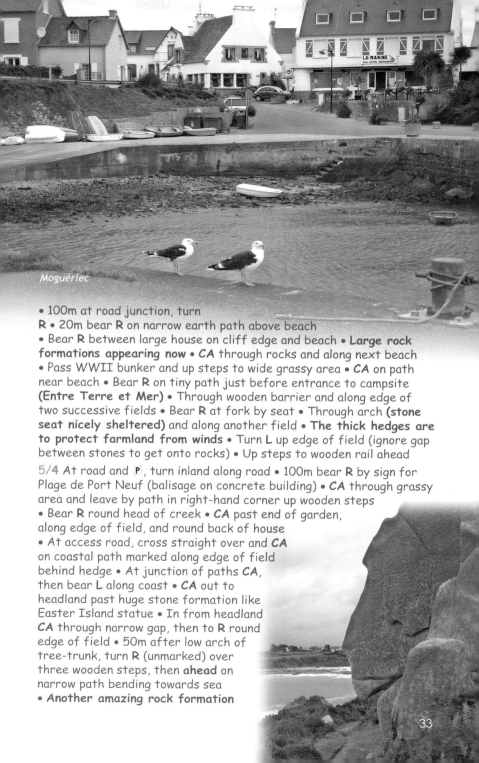

Moguériec

• 100m at road junction, turn
R • 20m bear **R** on narrow earth path above beach
• Bear **R** between large house on cliff edge and beach • **Large rock
formations appearing now** • *CA* through rocks and along next beach
• Pass WWII bunker and up steps to wide grassy area • *CA* on path
near beach • Bear **R** on tiny path just before entrance to campsite
(Entre Terre et Mer) • Through wooden barrier and along edge of
two successive fields • Bear **R** at fork by seat • Through arch **(stone
seat nicely sheltered)** and along another field • **The thick hedges are
to protect farmland from winds** • Turn **L** up edge of field (ignore gap
between stones to get onto rocks) • Up steps to wooden rail ahead

5/4 At road and **P**, turn inland along road • 100m bear **R** by sign for
Plage de Port Neuf (balisage on concrete building) • *CA* through grassy
area and leave by path in right-hand corner up wooden steps
• Bear **R** round head of creek • *CA* past end of garden,
along edge of field, and round back of house
• At access road, cross straight over and *CA*
on coastal path marked along edge of field
behind hedge • At junction of paths *CA*,
then bear **L** along coast • *CA* out to
headland past huge stone formation like
Easter Island statue • In from headland
CA through narrow gap, then to **R** round
edge of field • 50m after low arch of
tree-trunk, turn **R** (unmarked) over
three wooden steps, then **ahead** on
narrow path bending towards sea
• **Another amazing rock formation**

33

FOURS À GOÉMON

On top of the dunes here is a seaweed oven or four à goémon. In a ditch lined with stones and divided into compartments, the dried seaweed was burnt until blocks of soda were left. These were sold to a chemical factory at Pont Christ in the first half of the 20th century. For more on this process and the manny uses of seaweed see p. 83.

5/5 At wide hard track and P at head of bay, go **ahead** and bear **R** onto track round coast • At P immediately take fork to **R** of toilet, along coast towards next point • Track narrows between two rocks • **Coast wilder and wilder, bay full of rocks curiously shaped** • From another P follow track above sandy beach, continuing on broad road • Where road turns inland, go ahead between two rocks • **CA** through another P (Port of Poulennou) and follow clear path over dunes **Exceptional rocks – one like a bird** to very large P with beach access to Plage de Rogguenic et des Amiets

5/6 From lifeguards' hut at An Amied (Les Amiets), **CA** along top of dunes above beach, passing to **R** of caravan/campsite • Approaching headland, bear **L** of houses • Follow road (becoming track) and bear **R** back toward coast • **View of stone Corps de Garde look-out at Lavillo, behind a large rock on the point**

• Cross gully and climb to grassy area • Bear **L** downhill on road and **R** at **TJ**

6/1 Follow road 1.5kms, through Kerfissien (bar/tabac, restaurant) - **CA** where D330 turns away to Plouescat, **CA** past another road inland

6/2 Where road finally turns left, **CA** along top of beach 50m to narrow path over headland • Behind large rock, **CA** on wider path joining from left • 150m bear **R** onto track • At road, turn sharp **R** back toward coast • **CA** to P at end

6/3 To **L** of driveway, follow track down **R** edge of field • At end bear

CORPS DE GARDE DE AMIETS

This little guardhouse, only big enough to house three or four look-out men, was part of a chain of signal posts to warn of the approach of enemy ships. Another of these look-outs at Lavillo was built between 1730 and 1740 on a site recommended by Vauban (see p.96) in 1690. It was intentionally hidden from the sea behind a large rock.

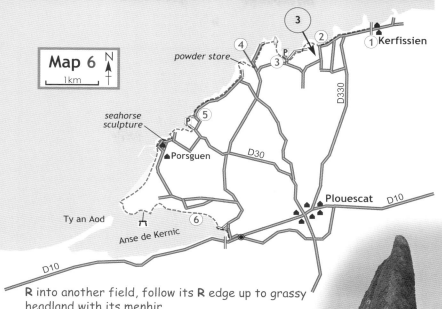

Map 6 N ↑
1km

Kerfissien ①
② ③
powder store
④ ③ P
D330

seahorse sculpture
P ⑤
▲Porsguen
D30

Plouescat D10

Ty an Aod ⌂
⑥
Anse de Kernic

D10

R into another field, follow its **R** edge up to grassy headland with its menhir

MENHIR OF CAM LOUIS This Neolithic standing stone is nearly 7m tall. There is a local legend that hidden treasure is concealed here, but it can only be reached during the midnight chimes of Christmas day. The name means 'Lame Louis'.

• Past menhir, don't follow path onto beach, but go to **L** of hedge for 50m to track • Follow track (becoming road) 500m

6/4 Where road turns inland, turn **R** on narrow path behind hedge • **CA** along field edge, past powder store, and out to headland • Follow path inland on track, becoming little road, between houses • Follow 1km, bearing **R** and **ahead** at junction **(One can turn down a grassy track to be by the sea about half way and climb out onto the headland cut off by houses – get back onto the road from**

Just to the left of the path at St-Eden is an 18th century powder store, now missing its roofing stones. This served a nearby battery as part of the coastal defences against attacks primarily from the English.

other end over a bank)
• Road comes back to
shore at another bay - **CA**
on road

6/5 After road goes
inland, turn sharp **R** along
path around next headland
• Follow round above
beach in front of houses
and caravans • Through  P
follow rough road inland to
head of creek, then sharp
R onto track, bearing **R**
again immediately between
two boulders to go out

This seahorse statue once stood by the church in Plouescat, but so missed its natural environment that it was transferred to this spot. It was fashioned from granite for an exhibition in 1989 by sculptors Patrig Ar Goarnig and Lucien Crenn.

onto headland • Before road and houses, bear **R** across grass and go in
front of houses onto edge above rocky beach • Cross open grassy area
back onto road • Turn **R** along road • **Pretty little sandy beach here
enclosed by rocks** • At junction just ahead, go **R** onto coast road past
seahorse statue

• **ALTERNATIVES**: Where road turns **L**, **EITHER** go **R** and down steps
to digue, then make your way **L** along beach, passing in front of centre
nautique (toilets outside) to harbour at Porsguen. **OR** follow road
between houses to end, then turn **R** to harbour • **Another memorial
plaque for the Athabaskan losses can be seen here (see p.30)**

• **CA** across wide P to narrow path on grass above beach • Cross tiny
tarmac track and keep going on narrow path over dunes • Walk along
sandy beach (Bar here) or **CA** on dunes • **Bathing here** • **If you want
to cut off the point, look for road through houses to left and you
will be able to see the other side of this promontory and cross
straight over to it - but it's worth continuing out to the point
(seats) for the great views of the estuary, Keremma sands and Ty
an Aod. Strong currents in the estuary – no bathing or trying to
wade across** • **CA** round headland to P and moorings • A little further
on is beach with alley grave • **This is an area of striking and curious
natural rock formations** • Go on beach or follow paths above water
• Path eventually becomes track, crosses little access road and

ALLÉE COUVERTE DE GUIRNIVIT

The position of this neolithic burial site directly on the beach is unusual. With a change of sea level of approx. 7-10 metres in the last five thousand years, the alley grave is now under water at high tide. Excavations showed the chamber to have been used for collective burials, and finds included arrow heads, polished axes and fragments of pottery. Many stones, including the roof coverings, are now missing, possibly taken for the nearby jetty used by seaweed collectors, but the surrounding precinct is still clear.

continues as grassy path • Keep near water, passing in front of a sailing centre • A few paces on road, then **L** between hedges to continue along top of beach, then along raised sandy bank above marshes

6/6 Where path divides, go **R** along top of grassy bank (not well walked, but path exists) • Soon there is water on both sides - at end, bear **R** down to top of marshes – very wet and muddy (NB at high tide, use fields above) • At a track, go ahead then **R** at fork • At road. turn **R**, then bear **R** again over little stone bridge • Turn **R** along main road (D10)

DIVERSION: To go into Plouescat for shops and services, turn left along the front of the casino and continue ahead for 1.5kms

Plouescat is a small town of character, centred around the 16th century halles (covered market), the oldest surviving in Finistere. The market is on Saturday mornings.

2. PRACTICAL INFORMATION

SHOPS & SERVICES

- **Roscoff** TO 02 98 61 12 13 www.roscoff-tourisme.com Mkt Wed
- **Plouescat** TO 02 98 69 62 18 www.tourisme-plouescat.com Mkt Sat
- **Santec** www.santec.fr Mkt Sat

ACCOMMODATION

Chambres d'hôte

1. **Ty Glaz Du** (200m) 295 route de Poulmavic, 29250 Santec
   02 98 29 41 60 www.tyglazdu.com
2. **Annaik Moal** (on route) 435 rue du Port, Moguériec, 29250 Sibiril
   02 98 29 99 79 Open all year
3. **Jacqueline & Thierry Marical** (300m) Prat-Bian, 29430 Plouescat
   02 98 61 97 27 www.pratbian.info Open all year

Gîte d'étape/Rando Gîte

4. **Rando Gîtes des Deux Rivières** (1km, Anse du Guillec) Le Bourg,
   29250 Plougoulm 02 98 29 90 63 laplougoulmoise@orange.fr

Camping

5. **Camping Village de Roguennic** (on route) 29233 Cléder 02 98 69 63 88
   www.campingvillageroguennic.com Overnight in caravan possible.
6. **Camping Le Theven** (Entre Terre et Mer) (on route) 29250 Sibiril
   02 98 29 96 86 http://pagesperso-orange.fr/camping.theven.29
   Open all year

TRANSPORT

Taxi

Armor Taxi - Roscoff 02 98 69 70 67 / 06 62 21 72 00

Michel Buzaré - Cléder 02 98 19 48 84 / 06 62 09 50 29

Taxis Calarnou - Plouescat 02 98 29 51 95 / 06 25 67 40 70

OTHER WALKS

Roscoff has two well-marked circuits of 7 and 12kms, the latter (blue balisage) going around most of the peninsula.

There is also a linear walk of 6kms to the Perharidy promontory.

3.Plouescat-Plouguerneau
Pays Pagan
47 kms

The names Pays Pagan, Côtes des Légendes and Côte des Naufrageurs (Wreckers' Coast) have all been applied to this area. This form of identity is largely for tourist purposes these days, but the granite rocks of this coast are formidable and it is not hard to imagine the frequency of shipwrecks here. The term 'pagan' (from paganus=country-dweller in Latin) has often been used by outsiders to denote a certain wildness of terrain and inhabitants!

This section provides easy walking beside many fine beaches and a marshy estuary, before the final stretch along cliffs. It is worth paying a visit to the Maison des Dunes at Keremma to discover the environmental significance of an exceptional area. Bird-watchers will find plenty of interest both here and on the Etang du Curnic beyond Guissény. The area is good for swimming, and I also recommend a pause at Meneham. A few years ago this was a ruined hamlet of fishermen's cottages, but it has now been restored with careful attention to traditional practices.

THE DUNES OF KEREMMA

This magnificent 6km stretch of sandy beach and dunes has been shaped by the winds, tides and currents over a long period of time. The western end by the Etang (lake) de Goulven is somewhat sheltered from those weather conditions which have thrown up a long spit of sandbank to the east at the entrance of the Bay of Kernic. Behind the littoral, an area of polder (low-lying land reclaimed from water by a system of dykes and channels) was formed in the early 19th century, largely by the efforts of local landowner, Louis Rousseau, who used the name Ker-Emma after that of his wife. Careful management now supports the dunes, with orpines, couch and marram grasses stabilising the sand as their long roots form a mesh below ground. Marsh-harriers hunting over this area are a common sight. Behind the dunes, where a footpath runs, more than 15 types of orchid flourish, and creeping thyme and euphorbia proliferate as ground cover. In addition to human usage, very active warrens of rabbits help to keep the vegetation in check.

This combination of sea, dune, lake and marsh is a haven for birds and the Bay of Goulven is an important ornithological reserve. From migratory Siberian geese to sand-pipers and golden or ringed plovers, there are thousands of birds to be seen here at all times of year: black-tailed and bar-tailed godwits arrive at the beginning of summer, whilst spoonbills winter at Penn ar C'hleuz, an area sheltered by reefs.

A circuit of 4.5kms from the Maison des Dunes, including Lac de Goulven, Penn ar C'hleuz and the dunes is recommended for keen bird-watchers. Please remember this is a fragile ecological environment and keep to the paths.

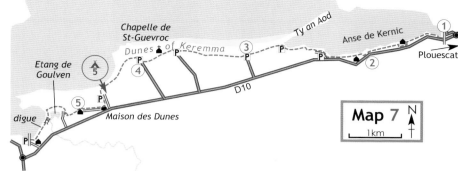

DIRECTIONS

7/1 Turn **R** along main road D10, with footpath on grassy bank on right • At buildings return to road briefly, bear **R** through lay-by back onto bank

The long sandy spit of Ty an Aod is clearly visible across the water. The name means 'house on the edge/shore' but this has now been destroyed.

7/2 Where D10 swings away, and path joins sandy track, bear **R** then **L** to continue by water • Keep **R** of house • At 🅿 by D10 again, bear **R** down track • **CA** to dunes of Keremma • Cross little bridge to large 🅿 and turn **R** towards sea

ALTERNATIVES: EITHER walk along the magnificent beach as far as point 7/4 **OR** follow footpath behind **(rather than on dunes, in the interests of protecting a fragile environment)**

7/3 Follow path through next 🅿 • 80m fork **R** (marked Chapel St-Guevroc) • From next 🅿 take sandy track behind dunes, passing to **L** of Chapelle St-Guevroc • **CA** to next 🅿

CHAPELLE ST-GUEVROC

St-Guevroc (Kirec or Guirec) came from Wales in the 6th century as a follower of St-Tugdual. A hermit, he was associated with various places in the Trégor region further east, as the place names Locquirec and Perros-Guirec reflect.

The chapel on this site in medieval times was abandoned and eventually lost under the sands. Rediscovered in 1869, a fresh water spring under the choir reached by a little staircase of 13 steps was found. Originally the chapel was surrounded by a cemetery – a 12th century coin indicated the antiquity of the site.

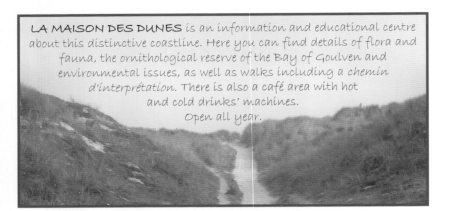

LA MAISON DES DUNES is an information and educational centre about this distinctive coastline. Here you can find details of flora and fauna, the ornithological reserve of the Bay of Goulven and environmental issues, as well as walks including a chemin d'interprétation. There is also a café area with hot and cold drinks' machines.
Open all year.

7/4 Bear **R**, diagonally across P to track lined with short wooden posts • Where path divides go **L** • Keep **R** of chain link fence • Level with portacabin on top of dunes, bear **L** to P • **CA** to *Maison des Dunes* • Follow wooden walkway to **R** of *Maison des Dunes*. **A series of information panels on the route gives the history of the landscape**

7/5 Bear **R** of buildings and **ahead** through wooden barrier • 200m go **R** then **L** to join track • Turn **R** along track round little lake (Etang de Goulven) • On far side climb bank to view Baie de Goulven. **Depending on tide times, it is possible to walk right across to Plounéour-Trez** • Go **L** along top of bank, cross bridge onto digue • At far end, turn **R** by tree stump • Follow narrow path to P

8/1 Through P **CA** alongside bay • Turn **L** onto track • Before road turn **R** in front of buildings • Through P follow track beside bay • At road, turn **R** 20m then **L** to continue along former railway

Etang de Goulven

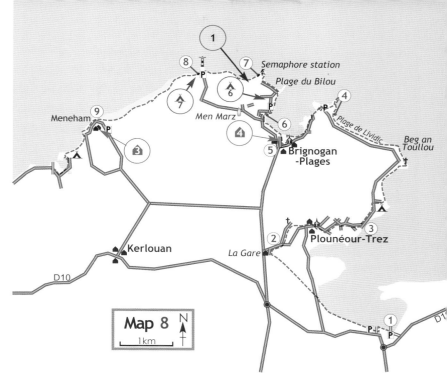

- At buildings continue to just before station (La Gare) and turn sharp R across yard, follow road to **TJ**, turn **R**

The narrow gauge railway came from Landerneau via Lesneven. This section, opened in 1894, was extended to Brignogan Plages in 1901. Like many similar rural services it was known as *le petit train patate* (the little potato train).

8/2 250m turn **L** • 200m, before cross, go **R** at far corner of garden wall • Follow to bear **L** onto main road into Plounéour-Trez • In centre, turn **R** then **L** to pass behind mairie • **CA** through garden and down steps • turn **L** into alleyway • At end of church bear **R** down little road • Bear **R** again and ahead 125m • Turn **L** onto Route de Creac'h ar Beuz • At crossroads turn **R**, then fork **L** • Follow road down to coast

8/3 Turn **L** on road 500m • At Crêperie de Kerurus turn **R** • Through P bear **L** on path over dunes • Halfway round bay, bear **R** onto road but leave it again to walk out over grassy point (cross on headland) • **CA** along dunes, away from road

ALTERNATIVE: from Beg an Toullou walk right along the beach

8/4 Cross end of beach to path over grassy headland • Return to bear **R** on track reaching road beside P • Turn **R**, follow road **L** and ahead onto beach • 100m go **L** on slipway • Follow access road to main road by harbour wall • Turn **R** along front • At far end, turn **R** down passage

MEN MARZ

400m from the coast is an 8m high neolithic menhir, later christianised by the addition of one cross on top and one carved on the face. A fertility rite involved tossing coins onto its protruding ledge. The name Men Marz means 'Miracle Stone', a reference to the legend that St-Pol (see p.23) turned the sea back from this spot.

behind restaurant • Follow beach **L** 100m • Turn **L** up steps • **CA** through churchyard to turn **R** on road • Follow up to *centre bourg* (mairie and La Poste on left, Presse/bar opposite)

8/5 Follow little road to **R** of pink *Office Notarial* • **Pass gîte d'étape** • Turn **L** along beach • 100m sharp **L** up slipway • Turn **R** onto road • 200m follow **R** • At **L** bend go **ahead** on rue de Keravezan **OR** turn **L** and in 100m bear **R** for **DETOUR** to Men Marz(400m). Return by same route • Go **R** of Café du Port and follow lane **ahead**

8/6 At road go **R** • **CA** to P • Near far corner, bear **R** toward beach • Turn **L** along wide track • Through wooden barrier continue over top of *centre nautique* • Through another barrier,follow path down to road, bear **R** • Turn **L** along *Promenade du Bilou*, alongside beach with large rock formations • Road narrows to footpath, **CA**, then **R**, between Semaphore Station and rocky beach

SEMAPHORE STATION This maintains 24 hours surveillance of sea and sky from the île de Vierge to the île de Batz. Sophisticated equipment monitors security, distress calls, pollution threats and provides severe weather warnings.

8/7 CA along dunes, passing behind house on shore • Keep **R** of large apartment complex - stay by beach • Path becomes sandy track – At 90° **L** turn, **CA** by beach • At lighthouse turn **L**, then ahead through P to little path ahead between rocks

Café du Port

THE LIGHTHOUSE OF PONTUSVAL, built in 1869, provides a link in the chain between those at the île de Vierge and île de Batz on this treacherously rocky coast.

guardhouse

gîtes

MENEHAM

Meneham is dominated by huge rocks enclosing a tiny look-out or guardhouse (1695), part of Vauban's coastal defensive system in the late 17th century, later used by customs' officers trying to catch smugglers. The village, once the home of fishermen and seaweed workers, was left a deserted ruin in the 20th century. It was like that when I first saw it five years ago, but has now been restored with regard for original methods and materials. The main thatched building is an auberge, and one row of cottages has been made into gîtes, with flexible accommodation (including a dormitory) and excellent facilities – perfect for walkers on the coastal path. A traditional baker's oven provides daily bread, and artisans' workshops are also helping to bring new life to the site. The reception cottage has an exhibition and video. See www.meneham.com for details and booking.

drying seaweed

8/8 Follow through arch of trees • **CA** 2kms above beach, with occasional diversions through Ⓟs, passing a seaweed oven (see p.79), and at one point bearing **R**, down steps, over little bridge, then **L** onto dunes again. **Massive rocks of Meneham are visible ahead** • At fork in path go **R** to continue above beach or **L** to cross Ⓟ to Meneham

8/9 CA on coastal path, **past seaweed oven and stacks of drying seaweed. Shortly after, guardhouse to left between huge rocks (see above)** • **CA** along top of dunes, with road alongside. **The walking here is easy on a wide sandy or grassy path along another immense sandy bay** • Follow path **L** along edge of creek on grassy dyke, with marshes on left **(As an alternative, at low tide it is possible to make one's way along the beach by wading through the creek)** • At end, go up to road, bear **R** across bridge • **CA** ahead through houses 175m, then turn **R** towards coast

9/1 **CA** through P⃞
(with option of
going out to end of
rocky promontory
before heading on
above beach) • **CA**
along dunes,
across access
tracks and P⃞s for
3.5kms • **Beautiful
boulder and rocky
island strewn
coast** • Brief
detour around lifeboat
station (at 2kms) is necessary
(toilets here). There are also
WWII bunkers set in the dunes from time to time. If one deep gully
presents a difficulty there is a bridge a little way to the left.

9/2 Path ends on little road: bear **R** along it 200m, then turn off to **R**
• Follow path nearest beach, bearing **R** past bunker • Go down steps to
cross access road • At P⃞, bear **L** (although it's possible to go **R** out
round promontory if desired and tide permits) • Continue nearest to
edge of beach, round little cove, before turning **L** inland to cut out
small headland • Go ahead on road or dunes • Where road bends inland,
CA on narrow footpath, soon between rocky beach and houses • **CA**
through section of steps, hedges and rocks to fenced path clearly
marked • **Guissény church comes into view ahead** • Follow path of
rough stones along beach • **CA** on sand for 100m to steps • Then turn

Map labels: Enez Croaz-Hent, Dibennou, Etang du Curnic, Guissény, D10, Map 9, N, 1km

R along path again, bearing **R** at
fork soon after, along very edge
of dunes • Follow briefly onto
beach then up steps **The route
is now following the estuary**

Guissény marshes

9/3 At road turn **R** and follow
400m • At junction turn **R** down
signed footpath • Turn **L** up
steps just before beach • **CA**
along estuary to where path
turns inland to a track, cross it
and ahead 30m to signed path to
R • By little beach, go **R** for a
short distance on road, then back
R (signed), continuing between marshes and vegetable fields • At
track, continue ahead, then **R** at little road • 250m just after S-bend,
go **R** • Returning to estuary, go **L** on overgrown banked path alongside
marshes

9/4 At end of path, go **L** to road D10 • Follow **R** 50m
• Turn **R** after mill (**chambres d'hôte**) • Follow coast path
alongside fields, then down steps onto track by estuary
• At road, go **R**, then **L** through **P**, past dolphin sculpture
• **CA** along back of college • **CA** through college buildings,
then along access road • Turn **R** at road, then **L** along path
by water, passing stone cross on bank • Follow path inland
to road, follow **R** 60m, then path **R** back to the coast
• Past extraordinary Barrachou rocks, **CA** around three
headlands (lookout/customs house on third headland) and
out to Pointe de Dibennnou • **CA** round point to barrage
• Follow raised path along barrage, Étang du Curnic
(plentiful bird-life) on left • At end bear **R** to follow path
around headland

10/1 ALTERNATIVES: At start of causeway to Enez Croaz-Hent
EITHER walk along beach, as far as point 10/2 **OR**
cross **P** and continue along top of dunes • Keep to
path between fences

Barrachou rocks

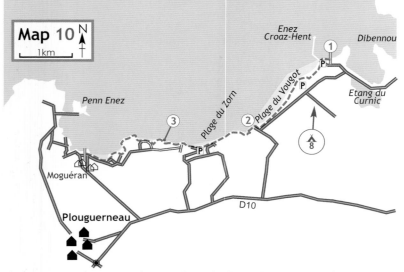

where required • At road towards end of beach turn **R** • Follow access road down to sand

10/2 Follow beach **L** 75m then climb right hand side of gully **(bit of a scramble but it is the right path)** to grassy path rising on **R**, pass over headland • Where path divides go **R (Plage du Zorn comes into view)** • At tarmac road follow ahead 20m, turn **R** on narrow path down towards beach • *CA* through P to road • Follow **R** down to beach • Turn **L** along beach to path over headland • Here bear **R** on path nearer clifftop • *CA* on narrow path along top of cliff, then high above another little beach

10/3 On far side continue around headland toward another beach • Ignore path from beach, continue to track • Turn **R** along track down to beach • *CA* on road from beach • As it rises, fork **R** on grassy path • Halfway through tunnel of bushes, fork **R** • Follow round field, continue past end of hedge, down towards another beach • Ignore path down to sand, bear **L** behind beach on sunken path • Before road, bear **R** on path • Follow round headland • Bear **R** ahead on road to **TJ** • Turn **R** along road behind beach at Moguéran

Plage du Vougot

3. PRACTICAL INFORMATION

SHOPS & SERVICES
- **Plouescat** TO 02 98 69 62 18 www.tourisme-plouescat.com Mkt Sat am
- **Plounéour Trez** TO 02 98 83 45 03 www.ot-plouneourtrez.com
- **Brignogan Plages** TO 02 98 83 41 08 www.ot-brignogan-plage.fr
  Summer mkt Fri
- **Guisseny** TO 02 98 25 67 99 www.Guissény.cotesdeslegendes.com

ACCOMMODATION
Chambres d'hôte
1. Odile Berthoule (100m) La Terre du Pont, Rue du Rocher de l'Eléphant, 29890 Brignogan-Plage 02 98 83 58 49 www.terredupont.com
2. Moulin du Couffon (on route) 29890 Kerlouan 02 98 25 78 43 www.moulinducouffon.com

Gîte d'étape
3. Meneham (on route) 29890 Kerlouan 02 98 83 99 78 www.meneham.com
4. Brignogan Plages (on route) 5 rue Goulven Pont, 29890 Brignogan Plages 02 98 83 41 08

Camping
5. (Municipal) Ker Emma (on route) 29430 Treflez 02 98 61 62 79
6. Camping Côte des Légendes (on route) Keravézan, BP36, 29890 Brignogan-Plages 02 98 83 41 65 www.campingcotedeslegendes.com
7. Camping du Phare (on route) Plage du Phare, 29890 Brignogan-Plages 02 98 83 45 06 www.camping-du-phare.com
8. Camping du Vougot (500m) 29880 Plouguerneau 02 98 25 61 51 www.campingplageduvougot.com

TRANSPORT
Taxi: Taxi Calarnou 02 98 29 51 95 / 06 25 67 40 70 Plouescat
Taxi Calonnec 02 98 83 96 35 Guissény

OTHER WALKS
Keremma - The Maison des Dunes has details of local walks, including a *chemin d'interprétation*

Guissény - 10km circuit including coastal path and marshes. See *Walking and other Activities in Finistere*

Plounéour Trez - 8km circuit, yellow and green balisage. Depart from Museum of Local Traditions

Brignogan Plages - Circuit du Phare, 6kms, yellow balisage. Depart from TO or Lighthouse Pontusval. Includes menhir and Chapelle Pol

MEGALITHS

Finistere is particularly rich in megaliths, the standing stones (menhirs) and burial places (dolmen/ allée couverte) of the new stone age, c.5000-2000BC. The southern-western tip around Penmarc'h was once the site of

Pors Poulhan

alignments as extensive as those at Carnac in Morbihan. Many stones have been broken, moved or simply lost in the development of agriculture and later settlements, but fortunately a significant number remain along the coastline, some only accessible on foot.

Although there is endless speculation about the significance and purpose of the menhirs, it will be clear to anyone walking the coastal path attentively that those positioned by the sea were placed as markers. (This is despite changes in sea levels since the Neolithic period, well illustrated by the alley grave of Guirnivit which is now underwater at high tide.) The similarity in appearance to many modern seamarks (concrete pillars) is striking. The menhirs would have functioned as signposts to seafarers, possibly as part of a series marking a route or as indicators of the location of important places or as territorial boundary marks. Often a large menhir on the cliff, such as that at Lostmarc'h, is close to an alignment or group of similar stones which were probably used as the focus of ceremony and ritual in a religious context. In this case it may be pointing the way for travellers arriving to join in the celebrations.

Alternatively it may highlight the placing of an important dolmen nearby. As the burial places were most likely related to families or clans, the significance of the menhir might be territorial or minatory, staking a claim to land for a particular group or tribe. Sometimes the burial places themselves are positioned so as to be seen clearly from the sea: at the end of the Pointe de la Torche in the Baie d'Audierne, for example, there is a large dolmen, and at Ménez Drégan a whole necropolis stands outlined on the headland.

Neolithic man may have been the first to settle on the land, cutting down trees and cultivating crops, but he was also a seafarer, as we know from evidence of goods traded all over Europe. Axe-heads and unpolished stone from Brittany have been found as far afield as Belgium, England and the south of France. Certainly plenty of wood was available for sailing craft, whether in the form of rafts, coracles or canoes. Archaeologists believe that the huge stones raised as menhirs or used in constructing dolmens were sometimes transported by water from their place of origin, strapped beneath rafts. It is possible that the actual shape of some burial chambers is that of an inverted boat, perhaps connecting to beliefs current at the time about the soul travelling to another world across water, led by a psycho-pomp or spirit guide.

Le Musée de la Préhistoire at Penmarc'h holds over 3000 artefacts from all the major sites in Finistere (see p.162).

4. Plouguerneau-Lampaul-Ploudalmézeau
The Abers

64 kms

The region of the Abers combines some magnificent, easy coastal walking with two large wooded estuaries, Aber Wrac'h and Aber Benoît. The seascape here consists of often rocky bays, grassy dunes and low headlands. The views to thin offshore islands, 'comet's tail' streaks of rock and the lighthouse of île Vierge are impressive, whilst the wild atmosphere around the archaeological site of Beg-Monom particularly sticks in my memory.

The Abers themselves provide a variety of scenery, differing considerably between the wide waterways of high tide and the exposed channels of low tide, when the dual composition of sandy flats and marshland is apparent. The route also passes through the coastal villages of L'Aber Wrac'h and St-Pabu, popular sailing centres in high season. The attractive town of Plouguerneau, with its services and excellent seaweed museum, is easily accessible from several points. Chapels, a 'lost' graveyard, and a neolithic alley grave provide interesting religious remains.

CHAPEL and ORATORY of ST-MICHEL Le NOBLETZ

Paths on the left lead up to this chapel, 150m off the coast path, with the little spire just visible over the brow of the hill. Michel le Nobletz, born in nearby Plouguerneau in 1577, was a Breton missionary who taught the scripture stories to illiterate peasants by means of painted 'maps' (taolennou) on wood or sheepskin. Some representations of these can be seen here when the chapel is open in the summer months.

Oratory

PLOUGUERNEAU The Musée des Goémoniers et de L'Algue (open April - Sept) is a fascinating exhibition of the history of the seaweed industry, evoking the atmosphere of earlier times and illustrating the adaptations which have enabled it to continue to flourish today.

DIRECTIONS (see map opposite)
(Access to Plouguerneau from here, 2kms by road)
11/1 Follow road from behind beach at Moguéran 500m, turn **R** at crossroads • 200m to junction, then **CA** on little road between chalets • At end, **CA** on beach: halfway along, go **L** up to concrete fence, follow it **R** • At access road follow **L**, at road turn **R** • Follow main road **R** (refreshments) down to Ⓟ and turn **R** • 50m turn **L** through wooden barrier
DETOUR: For a short detour around Penn Enez (where there is a 17th century maison de garde now used for exhibitions), **CA** down the road and return to this point
• Follow path around next headland 1.75km to La Grève Blanche, passing spectacular rock formations and paths on **L** to chapel and oratory of St-Michel le Nobletz (see above)
DETOUR: from La Grève Blanche to Iliz Koz (see below)
11/2 Turn **R** over dunes between beach and Ⓟ (lighthouse on Île Vierge is soon visible far ahead) • Follow path inland behind house,

ILIZ KOZ

400m from the parking area is the extraordinary site of Iliz Koz, a parish close which was buried for centuries under sand. Graves now  uncovered date back to the medieval period, with fine engravings of ships, shields and swords and more mundane craftsmen's tools.

Ghostly remains of the church and graveyard can be visited at certain times or viewed over the fence.

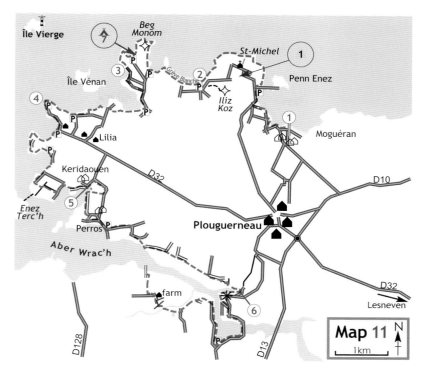

then go **R** down to beach, and **L** onto dunes again • Stay on path around rocky bay • Bear **R** at P and continue same path **L** round next cove (the route cuts out headland of Beg ar Spins) • At end, go **R** up road, becoming track after 50m • **CA** round headland • Where track divides, keep **R** • **Ahead are the huge rock formations of an éperon barré at Beg Monom** • At noticeboard, go **L** for shortcut or **R** to look

BEG-MONOM

The éperon barré, or fortified peninsula, was a defensive method employed in the Bronze and Iron Ages, and also found elsewhere in this part of Brittany. Here it is possible to see how man has made use of the natural contours of the land, together with a series of banks and ditches to isolate the point for a protected stronghold. The mound of earth and stone to the east of the largest rock formation was used as a look-out post. Worth looking at the views from it!

ÎLE VIERGE LIGHTHOUSE

This is the tallest lighthouse in Europe (82.5m), constructed at the end of the 19th century. There are nearly 400 steps inside (365 plus more to the lanterne), and more than 12,000 opaline plaques lining the walls to help neutralise the condensation problem. Nearby is a much smaller (33m) earlier (1845) lighthouse. It is possible to visit the island by boat in summer months. The ticket office for the Vedettes des Abers is further along the bay.

at archaeological site. Walk out to largest rock, then turn back before it to continue round coast • Path turns into track and joins road at Ⓟ • Bear **R** along another track round next headland

11/3 **CA** along road round top of bay, then **ahead** at junction • Follow road **L** • 250m at **TJ** go **R** • 350m just before next junction go **R** through Ⓟ on a track along top of bay • Path bears **L** to cut off headland • When it bears **R** and comes out on road, turn **L** • 50m go **ahead** on track • At fork soon after go **R** • **CA** round top of beach, then across part of beach and up slipway opposite (or round if tide is in) • At road go **R** 300m to Ⓟ, then take path **ahead** round coast (including about 30m around top of beach again) • Path ends by sculpture in parking area at 11/4

11/4 **CA** on road round bay (**ticket office for Île Vierge, and refreshments: hotel/restaurant and crêperie**) • Where road bends **L** inland, go **ahead** through Ⓟ and along top of beach 100m • Just past last house, go up rocks then **R** on path round bay • At fork at Ar Rest, bear **R** • Before slipway take path to **L** (or walk on beach) • **CA** along coast, bearing **R** to join track • Going inland, path splits then rejoins • Go across Ⓟ at head of beach and **ahead** over grass

The large island of ENEZ TERC'H ahead is accessible at low tide. It is also called the Île Américain, recalling its use during WWI as a base for American sea-planes combating German submarines along this coastline. A WWII concrete bunker also remains.

• At road follow 70m, then turn **R** along by beach • Follow track to road, **CA** • At end of road, turn **L** on green track • Soon after, turn **L** at **TJ** of paths, then follow 90° **R**, with views of Aber Wrac'h soon appearing • Go down to shore and turn **L** along road • 120m turn **R** along top of beach, take track on **L** before end • Follow same track along top of inlet

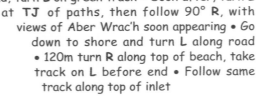

11/5 ALTERNATIVES: At Keridaouen (past road off to left)
AT LOW TIDE go **R** on track across marsh, bearing **R** round edge of
beach and then **ahead** to grassy track. **OR**, if the water is in, go on up
the road, then **R** and **R** again down to beach and **L** to join grassy track

• Follow track across fields to hamlet, and go
R at junction • 100m turn **L** by stone cross
• At bottom of road turn **R** and continue down
to port at Perros • By **P**, turn **L** uphill • Follow
500m to top, turn **R** (signed Ménez Perros)
• Downhill, 100m after **L** bend, turn **R** onto
narrow path down to water • Follow along top
of beach, then up track ahead • Towards top, at
L bend, fork **R** on narrower path • Joining track
at horseshoe bend, go **ahead** • At access road,
bear **R** and **ahead** on track. **This passes a sombre
sculpture of 1990 entitled 'Derediction' by
Bernard Sirven.** • 250m bear **R** downhill, dropping
steeply into valley • At **TJ** of tracks, go **R** downhill
and **ahead** at next junction (Access to Plouguerneau
from here - see map)

11/6 At road go **R** • Just past house (milin ar hoad) go **R**
along narrow footpath – **easy one to miss!** • Path goes
along creek, then inland • At road, go **L** uphill, then **R** at main
road, down to Pont du Paluden • Cross bridge over Aber Wrac'h

• Follow road to **P** of Relais de
l'Aber, turn **R** • **CA** on road for
almost 1km • Just before
gated end of road, fork **L** up
path • At top turn **R** • At
little road turn **L** 50m then **R**
onto wide path • **CA** past
lavoir, then down across
stream and turn **L** • Uphill at

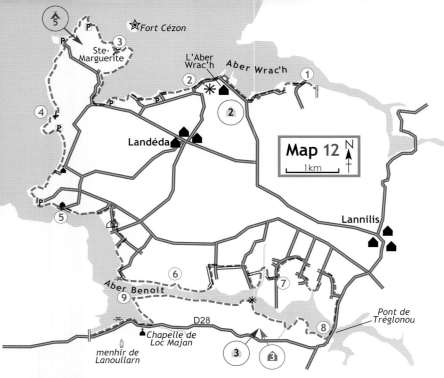

ABER WRAC'H

The word *aber* is of celtic origin (cf. placenames in Wales and Scotland) and signifies a tidal estuary. The meaning of *Wrac'h* here is less certain: it could come from the Breton for witch or old woman, or possibly the name of a fish (the vieille or *guurach*). Another idea is that it derives from the Aber du Pays d'Ac'h (aber being pronounced Ac'h in Breton).

The Aber Wrac'h, 2kms wide at the mouth, crosses eleven communes. It is navigable up to the Pont du Paluden, a length of 10kms. Further inland still are the remains of one of the oldest bridges in Brittany, the Pont du Diable, dating from the Gallo-Roman period.

FORT CEZON

A fort was constructed here by Vauban (see p.96) in 1694 to exploit the strategic position protecting the Aber W'rach, which was an important sheltered harbourage for naval and commercial shipping. The site was used in succeeding centuries for defensive purposes, right up to the German bunkers of WWII.

track, turn **R** (not sharp right) • At top of hill bear **L** at track junction, towards farm • By farm turn **L** on road • 100m **R** onto path between fields • 400m follow path **L** and down towards aber

12/1 At road, bear **L** • 100m turn **R** • At end of road **CA** on track/ path by shore • Path turns inland uphill: at top turn **R** on track, descending to aber again • **CA** to road, bear **R** • Follow to main road, bear **R** • Follow around harbour of L'Aber Wrac'h and ahead to port • Turn **R** into port and **L** along quay • At end, follow wall **L** to road • Turn **R**, follow road 600m beside water (viewpoint 100m uphill to L)

12/2 Where road turns inland, bear **R** along path above beach • At end go **ahead** up lane • Cross P and continue round top of bay • At **TJ** turn **R**, back towards water • Path just touches beach then goes straight back up between walls • Continue **ahead**, ignoring another track • At beach, go along top 100m, then **L** up steps • **CA** through P to road and turn **R** • Turn **R** again at junction • Follow road round top of bay **(past a memorial to the liberation of Landéda on 11 August 1944)** • Just before mini-roundabout bear **R** up lane (Sentier Pieton) • 100m, turn **R** up steps onto coastal path, follow ahead • **Fort Cézon is ahead on island which can be reached for 1-4 hours at low tide**

12/3 Through pine trees, join another track and go **R** • Follow briefly away from shore, then sharp **R** down side of house to beach • Leave it immediately up steps and continue **R** • Cross P and continue to **R** around headland (lookout post at the end and another a bit further on) • **CA** along dunes of St-Marguerite above beach, crossing P s and keeping ahead

12/4 Path finally leaves dunes and runs between hedges • At junction of paths turn **R** to go round next headland • Continue **R** through P along edge of bay, past chapel to **L** of path • Bear **R** along top of beach, and go **R** at picnic area • 400m, through barrier, go **ahead**, ignoring track uphill, keep by water • At mouth of Aber Benoit, turn

back **L** along wall above beach - Keep on path nearest estuary • After Ⓟ where road goes uphill, **EITHER** walk along beach, tide permitting, and up slipway past Viviers de Beg ar Vill **OR** go **R** along bottom of field then through ferns on narrow overgrown path, past warehouses at end

12/5 Up road 275m turn **R** on track downhill • **Ahead** along top of beach (If impassable, use narrow path just above on wall and then along edge of field, but beware electric fence. Rejoin beach eventually) • At road go **L** 300m up to junction • Go **R** here, and **R** again soon after • This little road drops down through hamlet with pretty lavoir and ugly manoir • At bottom go ahead up narrow road (route Delamare Deboutteville) • At next junction go **R** downhill back to aber • Follow No-Though-Road beside water • 80m path forks **R** onto beach • Stay on beach 300m then bear **L** up track • At bottom of road uphill L, bear **R ahead** on track • 200m to picnic area by water, **CA** through wooden barrier

12/6 After 1km at inlet, cross stream and go up steps • Follow path further 800m, then bear **L** on track uphill • Follow **R** and ahead to road • Bear **R** then **L** on another track • At road, turn **R**, follow down to aber • At bottom, turn **L** onto footpath just behind shore • At junction with track, bear **R** ahead • Cross stream and follow **R** to join track

12/7 At road turn **L** • Ignore two little roads on left, at fork bear **R**

PONT DE TREGLONOU

A wooden toll bridge of 1850 was the first fixed crossing here. Rebuilt in concrete in 1935, it was partly destroyed in WWII and then rebuilt. There is a very scenic picnic area is next to the bridge.

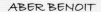

ABER BENOIT

The name of this estuary is probably a corruption of beniguet = blessed. Saint Majan and his father Tudgibus are said to have founded shrines on each side – at Loc Majan (see p.60) and Lothunou. The aber is 8kms long and served by a basin of 140km². Oysters of high quality are harvested here as they thrive on the plankton where salt and fresh water meet.

• At **TJ** turn **R** • **CA** 300m to crossroads, turn **L** • In Lothonou, where road bends R, turn **L** onto path • Follow down to creek, cross barrage and turn **L** up track • Go ahead at road • At crossroads go **R** • Follow road to **TJ**, turn **R** onto (busy) D28 • Follow 600m down to Pont de Tréglonou

12/8 Cross bridge and turn **R** immediately • Follow path above water between fields and trees • Cross head of creek and continue above aber • At next creek, cross stream and **CA**

(The tracks in this wood, grounds of the Manoir de Trouzilit, are used by the Pony Club based there. Keep to the path to the **R** of wooden barrier, alongside the track.)

• Pass fontaine on R, and later an hexagonal look-out on water's edge • At circular clearing, cross it ahead onto very narrow path and **CA** through wood, staying near water • Path emerges from woods before end of headland

12/9 At headland follow path **L** (but first take a few paces onto the point where is an overgrown seaweed oven - see p.79 - and three-way views of the estuary and St-Pabu across the water) • Follow narrow path ahead, Chapel of

Lookout

CHAPELLE DE LOC MAJAN

Majan was one of a host of holy men coming from Britain in the 6/7th centuries to the shores of Brittany. After landing near Brest with his father and other companions, Majan was attracted to this spot by a spring at the head of the estuary. Here he established a hermitage, chapel and fontaine. When he died, his body was buried beneath the choir of the earliest chapel. Various others have succeeded it, the current chapel, in the form of a Latin cross, dating mainly from the 17th century, although the west door is much earlier and there is also a chevet of 1771. The fontaine remains.

St-Majan is soon visible • Cross 🅿 to road and turn **R**, but keep behind bridge on narrow path away from road • Path runs parallel with D28 for some way – several connecting paths make it easy to cross road to visit chapel

• **CA** on path 1km between road and water, passing picnic tables with lovely views • Path comes up to road opposite mill, turn **R** (The Menhir de Lannoullarn is signed 1km to the **L** here by road)

13/1 Follow narrow grassy path alongside road across two bridges, then turn **R** along estuary • Follow **L** into wood to join small road on

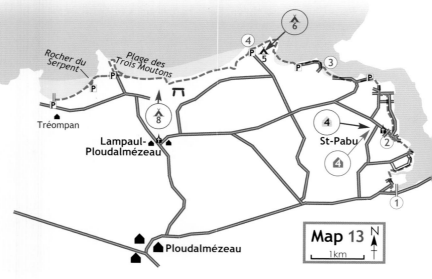

horseshoe bend • Follow road **R** 100m
to **L** bend • Turn **R** down grassy path
• Follow across head of creek and up
other side • At top, turn **R** down track
between houses • At road turn **R** then
L through wooden barrier 30m before
waterfront • Follow 250m bear **R** onto
road by wooden chalet • Follow road
to TJ, turn **L**

There is a crêperie in the attractive
old buildings opposite.

13/2 After 80m turn **R** up rue de
l'Aber Benoit

For refreshments, go on ahead a
short distance for a bar (Thalassa)
and bar/restaurant and public toilets near church

Seaweed oven

• **CA** 800m to **TJ**, turn **L** uphill • 200m turn **R** • 30m at fork bear **R**
ahead • Keep ahead at next junction, down to water and **CA** to **P**
• Turn **L** up road • 250m turn **R** and stay on road 250m • Bear **R** along
narrow path between hedge and wall, descending to sandy beach • **CA**,
then down steps to bear **L** on beach for 100m

13/3 Then **L** inland between concrete buildings • 30m fork **R** uphill and
go **R** along road at top • 650m in **P** go off to **R**, then turn **R** down
steps onto beach • 80m turn off beach, and at end of track bear **R**
round headland (passing well-preserved seaweed oven)

13/4 On reaching **P** at start of several kms of sandy beaches,
EITHER CA ahead on gravel track (coastal path) **OR** walk along sands
OR take one of many paths across dunes (but bear in mind dangers of
erosion)

**To the left is the spire of the church at Lampaul-Ploudalmézeau
and ahead is the beach of Les Trois Moutons (Three Sheep).
There is also a neolithic alley grave just behind the dunes. The
Allée Couverte du Ribl dates from c.3000BC.**

• Continue to end of
Plage des Trois
Moutons • At **P**
bear **L** and follow
track (left hand one
of three options) to
rejoin coast • Bear
L at two forks soon
after, then **L** along
by beach • Follow
path round first

Allée Couverte du Ribl

Rocher du Serpent

beach before large rock formation, Rocher du Serpent

ALTERNATIVES: EITHER Go directly to **L** of Rocher du Serpent on sandy path • At top, bear slightly **L** on boarded path • Go **R** before P, then along top of dunes (or on sandy track behind – but paths here not clear) **OR** - best idea would be along beach from Rocher du Serpent (balisage on bunker on beach)

• Come off beach by larger bunker, then over creek • **L** through P but sharp **R** by rock at end of P, before little road to **R**

4. PRACTICAL INFORMATION

SHOPS & SERVICES
- **Plouguerneau** TO 02 98 04 70 93 Mkt Thurs am
- **Lannilis** TO 02 98 04 05 43 www.abers-tourisme.com Mkt Wed
- **Lilia** • **Landéda**

ACCOMMODATION

Chambres d'hôte

1. Hélène Le Roux (>500m) Saint Michel, 29880 Plouguerneau
   02 98 04 62 16 Open all year
2. Marie-Jo Kersebet (120m)410 Mezedern, 29870 L'Aber Wrac'h
   02 98 04 92 57 Open all year

Chambres d'hôte + gîte d'étape

3. Manoir de Trouzilit (250m) Tréglonou, 29870 Lannilis 02 98 04 01 20
   www.manoir-trouzilit.com
4. M&Mme Dubois (200m) 54 rue de bourg, 29830 St-Pabu 02 98 89 87 35
   http://perso.orange.fr/dubois.jpm

Camping

5. Camping de Penn Enez (300m) 551 Ar Vourc'h, 29870 Landéda
   02 98 04 99 82 www.camping-penn-enez.com
6. Camping de L'Aber Benoit (200m) Corn ar Gazel, 29830 Saint-Pabu
   02 98 89 76 25 www.camping-aber-benoit.com
7. Snowland Loisirs (150m) Meledan, 29880 Plouguerneau 06 30 17 55 97
   www.snowlandloisirs.net
8. Municipal Camping Les Dunes (300m) Le Vourch, 29830 Lampaul-
   Ploudalmézeau 02 98 48 14 29 June-September

TRANSPORT

Vedettes des Abers 02 98 04 74 94 www.vedettesdesabers.com
   Boat trips to the Île Vierge or along the Abers
Taxi Quemener – Taxi des Abers 02 98 04 72 76 Plouguerneau
Taxi Abarnou 02 98 04 84 42 Landéda

OTHER WALKS

Landéda - 8km circuit of headland around chapel of St-Marguerite
Lannilis - 11 km circuit from Pont de Paluden, including coast, lavoir, old
railway track and Lannilis

5.Lampaul-Ploudalmézeau -Pointe St-Mathieu

Pays d'Iroise

68 kms

This fine walking territory begins with sandy beaches, dunes and low headlands, then circumnavigates the wooded haven of the Aber Ildut before building up to wilder, stark granite cliffs. It includes the most westerly point in France at Pointe du Corsen, which saw the only misty spell of my days here: the weather can certainly change very quickly on this Atlantic coast. The islands of Molène and even Ouessant in the Mer d'Iroise are visible in clear weather. Good paths characterise this area, even on the rather up and down later sections. Portsall, with its tragic Amoco Cadiz connection, and Lanildut, centre of the seaweed industry in northern Finistere, provide a focus for the economic development of the area - a sense of past prosperities and future potential. Le Conquet is the most picturesque of ports with its ancient architecture and lively harbour.

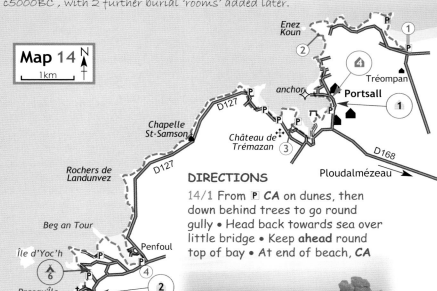

ÎLE CARN

Both 'carn' and the later 'cairn' signify a heap of little stones, the material used to construct these distinctive Neolithic funerary monuments. The large cairn on this island is a contemporary of the famous one at Barnenez. An original circular chamber dates to c5000BC, with 2 further burial 'rooms' added later.

Île Carn

Map 14 N
1km

Enez Koun

Tréompan

Portsall

anchor

D127

Chapelle St-Samson

Château de Trémazan

Ploudalmézeau

D168

Rochers de Landunvez

D127

Beg an Tour

Penfoul

Île d'Yoc'h

Presqu'Île du Vivier

Argenton

Presqu'Île St-Laurent

Pointe de Garchine

Porspoder

Mazou

D27

DIRECTIONS

14/1 From P **CA** on dunes, then down behind trees to go round gully • Head back towards sea over little bridge • Keep **ahead** round top of bay • At end of beach, **CA** on track and bear **R** on green path towards headland • At P, go **ahead** towards large rock formation at end • Continue round on path nearest edge

• Continue **R**, round top of dunes • At gully, go down and up again along top edge by the water • Go along wall in front of house, down steps, bear **R** towards beach, then **L** up steps on other side • Follow path out round next headland • At road, turn **R** 100m then **R** following clear path across grass • Bear **R** to go out round edge of next wild headland • **The island Enez Koun is ahead**

14/2 Turn inland just before first house • Go **R** at junction with another track, then **L** just after, returning to walk along beach • Go up steps at end and turn **L** • At road, bear **R** down a no-through road, becoming footpath • At end, go **L**, then **R** at fork • At junction, bear **R** ahead • 180m turn **R** along rue des pêcheurs • Follow to harbour (**To see the anchor of the *Amoco Cadiz* turn right**)

AMOCO CADIZ

In March 1978, the oil-tanker *Amoco Cadiz* foundered on rocks off the coast here in severe stormy conditions. Attempts to tug the ship into open water failed, and a ripped hull began the fatal spillage. Next day the ship broke in two, losing all 220,000 tons of crude oil. More than 300 kms of Breton coastline were eventually affected, with disastrous results for fishing, tourism and the environment. The ship's anchor is on the harbourside here as a reminder of this devastating 'marrée noire' or black tide.

• Turn **L** and follow road around harbour (**Refreshments and bakery here. On a cliff opposite is a stone cross - just behind is a Neolithic dolmen, which the path will pass**) • At end, bear **R** into ⓟ

DOLMEN OF GUILLIGUI

Situated on a headland with panoramic views, this site was used as early as the Mesolithic period as a base where weapons, notably arrowheads, were made. Around 6000BC it became a Neolithic burial place, with the dolmen still to be seen today. This was of side-entrance type, a form not common in Brittany, with a long chamber and one closed off cell. Upright stones surrounded the dolmen. A later Bronze Age tomb was added as successive generations used the site. The Christian monolithic cross from a local cemetery was put up in 1895.

• Take No Entry path in corner (to **L** of restaurant) • 100m turn **R** to dolmen of Guilligui and cross of Bar al Lan • *CA* past dolmen • Towards beach, bear **L** on track • At road, go **R** • 120m turn **R** down track, round head of creek • At road, *CA* • 250m at **L** bend go **ahead** on path, Chemin de Gwisselier

DETOUR: For Château de Trémazan continue **L** on road

CHÂTEAU DE TRÉMAZAN

The romantic ruins of this medieval castle are associated with the tragic story of two Breton saints, Tanguy and Haude. These two were brother and sister here, happy in childhood until their father remarried and the young man was sent away to court. Returning years later, Tanguy believed his step-mother's accusations against his sister and, in a rage, cut off her head. Haude picked it up again and placed it back on her shoulders before dying. Tanguy sought penance through pilgrimage and was pardoned by St-Pol before later becoming an abbot himself.

14/3 100m, at **TJ** of paths, turn **R** out onto headland • Through Ⓟ, bear **L** above beach • *CA* on open moorland • Through next Ⓟ *CA* on

CHAPELLE de ST-SAMSON (see next page)

Saint Samson was one of the seven 'founding' saints of Brittany. He arrived from south Wales in the 6th century and became bishop of Dol-de-Bretagne. This little chapel in his honour dates from 1785, although it was built in the previous century.

The simple interior has a painted altar and stained glass window of the healing saint. A fontaine just below was the focus for cures of rheumatism and eye problems. There was once a menhir on this site.

Rochers de Landunvez

narrow path parallel with road • Follow track **L** up into large **P** • **EITHER** go along beach and onto next headland, **OR** continue up road 175m, follow D127 **R** (Route touristique) then **L** towards sea, and just past **P**, turn **R** on path across grass • **CA** 1.5km to little chapel just left of path.

• **CA** on path to Pointe de Landunvez (the huge rocks on the point are an easy marker) • Follow path past Rochers de Landunvez and ahead bearing **R** (paths to **L** go off to the road) past further outcrops • Keep to path nearest edge of sandy inlet at Penfoul, around enclosure up to road (if tide is out, it is possible to cross sand to path clearly visible on other side) • Follow path just below road, along top of beach • At rough road, go **R** towards beach, then **L**

between hedges • At road, turn **L** briefly to **TJ**, then **R** • Follow 150m round to **TJ**, turn **R** • Turn **R** through **P** just before junction with D27

14/4 Take footpath to **R** of Argenton sign (**if water is high, just go on along road and turn right to join coastal path**) • At fork, go **R** and continue round beach, bearing **R** out towards point • Round head of cove, then carry on ahead through wooden barriers • Can walk out as far as Beg an Tour or cut across before first big rock • **CA** to road, turn **R** through **P** and **ahead** on road

• Road becomes track round next headland • At fork, go **R** past wooden barrier (**looking across to island of Île d'Yoc'h**) • Stay right by edge to see little powder store, otherwise go **ahead** to road and up **R** fork • Go through Ⓟ to far end, then **ahead** on footpath round bay

• Bear **L** at end, along the road • Bear **L** again at harbour - **Note stone cross on rock to right**; salon du thé (teashop) in ship moored at quay
• Bear **R** at main road to continue round Argenton harbour (Bakery and bar here at Argenton on front)

• At end of harbour wall, turn **R** on lane between houses • At Ⓟ go **R** on footpath • At dunes, carry on ahead • Cross road going out to Presqu'île-du-Viviers and **CA** over dunes (Many paths here – possible to follow road or beach instead) • Across road out to Presqu'île St-Laurent, **CA** on dunes • Take track to **R** of large sports building with bright mural (**Spire of Porspoder church ahead**) • Where track bends inland, go across dunes diagonally, between wooden posts
• Cross slipway of rocky bay, then **CA** on dunes • Follow path across rocks and over stream, then go **R** to continue (or **L** for short diversion up to church, worth seeing - see next page – also supermarket, bank, bar and post office)

SAINT BUDOC

In legend, Saint Budoc was the son of Aliénor or Azénor, who was falsely imprisoned by her father on account of jealous lies by her evil step-mother. She was condemned to death but the fires set to burn her refused to light, so she was shut up in the tower of the castle in Brest (see p.90) Finally she was thrown into the sea in a barrel, but survived the journey to Ireland where she gave birth to a son.

Budoc devoted himself to the religious life and came to Brittany in 585, landing in the bay here in a stone boat. After a year he moved to nearby Plourin and then to Dol-de-Bretagne where he became archbishop. His name - other versions include Buzeuc and Beuzec - allegedly comes from the Breton beuzet (drowned, or saved from drowning in this case!) but is probably rather from the old word in both Breton and Welsh 'budmael (victory + prince). An elaborate 18th century panel in the church here tells Budoc's story.

• Pass lavoir right by path soon after • At road, bear **R** along it • 100m **CA** on path • Table of orientation to left of path on grassy hillock • At fork of tracks, go **R**, then at another fork, bear **R** to go round headland (Pointe de Garchine) • Continue round another bay. (**Seaweed oven in garden of house by path**) • At Ⓟ, go **L** along road a few metres, then before first building bear **R** on path across grass • Follow round head of creek • **IF WATER IS HIGH**, exit to road here and follow **R** to **TJ**. Turn **R** and follow road down through Mazou to slipway, bearing **L** before it to **CA** on coastal path • **OTHERWISE**, cross wooden plank bridge, then go across top of pebbly beach, up

slipway and bear **R** to continue on coastal path

• Pass stone cross with its stone basin at Pen ar Gorred. The Île de Melon is opposite • Go **ahead** on beach for about 60m, then **L** up path • At little road turn **R** (Could go right across beach and up slipway opposite if tide is out) • Turn **R** at main road

15/1 At end of harbour, go **R** through Ⓟ and behind

Melon is named after an early Welsh/Cornish saint. In 1644 Henrietta María, the French wife of Charles I of England had to put ashore here with her young daughter in bad weather, before continuing to Paris via Brest.

Guérite de Melon

café/restaurant (**To the right is the Guérite de Melon, a 17th century look-out**) • Join road briefly, round top of beach • At end of bay, turn **R** through wooden barrier (marked dangerous because right on edge, but not very high and only for about 50m) Otherwise, go on up road 100m, then turn R. The two paths join • At road, go ahead 60m, then **R,** back on path • Go **R** and **R** to cross deep gully • At fork, take either path (passing another look-out house) • Cross P and **CA** on coast path

BATTERY OF ABER ILDUT

This 18th century construction served to defend the entrance of the Aber Ildut during the long-running naval conflicts between France and England. It consisted of two gun-platforms (for 12 pound canon), a small barracks, guardhouse and powder store.

• **CA** by water, past Rocher du Crapaud (Toad Rock) at end of stone jetty • At road, bear **R** along the harbour. **Bar/restaurant here. Boats to Ouessant from harbour in season.**

MAISON DE L'ALGUE This centre of interpretation has a mass of information about identifying, cultivating and making use of different types of seaweed. Models, films, photos and artefacts recall the traditional way of life of the Goémoniers and also present the up-to-date evolution of this important local industry. Open June to September.

• Past Maison de l'Algue, go up steps in front of diving building, then **ahead** through P • Stay on this path round head of creek • At end, go **L** up to road

Turn **R** and follow main road 900m through Lanildut to the church (good views of estuary and access to épicerie/bar/restaurant)

DETOUR: opposite church is the area of Le Rumorvan, where wealthy merchants and ship-owners once lived, when Lanildut was a port with international trading links. These fine houses of the 17/18th centuries are built of local granite, and some still have distinctive rounded chimney tops

• Turn down to the left of church, then at bottom of precinct go **ahead** on footpath • At fork turn **R**

15/2 Before beach, turn **L** through woods and continue along estuary for nearly 2 kms • Shortly after bridge over inlet, turn **L** up towards road (auberge here) • Just before road, turn **R** through barriers on path parallel to road (to circumvent the Manoir de Bel Air and its dovecote) • Cross track and go down to **R** along edge of field • Continue along estuary • Cross little stream on rocks, **CA** • Cross bridge by site of ancient mill • At Pont Rhun at head of estuary, turn **R** over bridge, then **R** again to rejoin path • Follow in and out, up and down through woodland according to lie of land • Stay on path nearest water and follow round heads of inlets, over little bridges: ignore paths off • At large P opposite Lanildut church, continue along track ahead 250m, then **R** along path on edge of fields **(There is a seaweed oven on R of path before turning down the long inlet)**

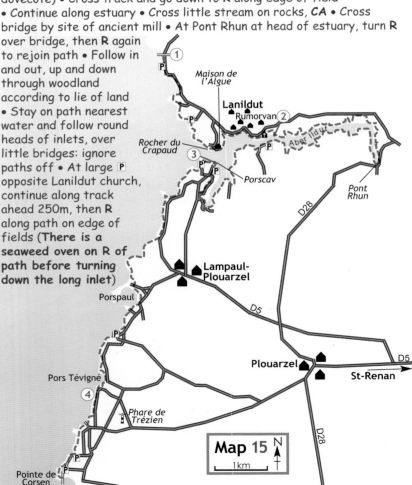

72

• Go **ahead** across little square (or go left briefly to see chapel of Dom Michel - see p.52), then out along no-through-road towards harbour (**Note the look-out point to the right. There was once a chapel here to Saint Christopher, patron of travellers; it was a focal point for prayers for those at sea, and a place to watch for the return of their ships**)

• Just before harbour go **L** up steps, then **R** along road • **CA**, soon above sand • Cross sliproad and turn **R** to continue along road that runs uphill above beach • At top, bear **L**, then down side of wall, continuing round headland • **As path begins to turn inland, there's a little round look-out tower to the right** • Before road, go **R** down steps, then ahead

16/5 Descend to another beach: go a few paces **L**, then **R** onto cliff • Follow road a few paces before bearing **R** again • At large ℗ (Porz Liogan) divert briefly along edge of road or go down to beach and up again • Keep **ahead** on path round headland of Pointe de Penzer, with Pointe St-Mathieu close ahead now

In the parking area at Porz Liogan is a simple granite menhir memorial to five RAF pilots whose plane was shot down on 6 July 1943 after a bombing raid on Brest. Four bodies were washed up and at first given a summary burial in the sand by the occupying forces. Local people, however, with help from the Germans about the location of mines on the beach, removed them for a blessing and burial at nearby Lochrist. A detachment of German soldiers attended the funeral to give a rifle salute in honour of Wing commander Owen, Flying Officer Swain, and Pilot Officers Long, Darbyshire and Ray.

5. PRACTICAL INFORMATION

SHOPS & SERVICES

Pays d'Iroise Tourism TO 02 98 84 41 15 www.vacanceseniroise.com
• **Portsall**
• **Porspoder** www.porspoder.fr
• **Lampaul-Plouarzel** (TO 02 98 84 04 74) www.lampaul-plouarzel.fr
• **Lanildut** www.pagesperso-orange.fr/lanildut/
• **Le Conquet** TO 02 98 89 11 31 www.leconquet.fr Mkt Tue am

ACCOMMODATION

Chambres d'hôte

1. Mme Menesguen (on route) 02 98 49 40 13 45 rue du Port, 29830 Lampaul-Ploudalmézeau
2. André Sénac (100m) 02 98 89 42 30. 2 Impasse Avel vor, 29840 Argenton en Landunvez. andre.senac@aliceadsl.fr
3. Mme Annick Pastouret (100m) 8 rue Amiral Guépratte, 29217 Le Conquet 02 98 89 14 25

Gîte d'étape

4. Gîte d'étape (on route) 29 rue du port, Portsall, 29830 Ploudalmézeau 02 98 48 10 48 www.Ploudalmézeau.fr Open all year

Rando-gîte

5. Village Vacances Beauséjour (500m) Parc de Beauséjour, 29217 Le Conquet 02 98 89 09 21 www.lesvillagesmer.com

Camping

6. Municipal Camping St-Gonvel (on route) St-Gonvel, 29840 Landunvez 02 98 89 91 02 www.landunvez.fr
7. Camping des Blancs Sablons (300m) Le Théven, 29217 Le Conquet 02 98 89 06 90 www.lescledelles.com

TRANSPORT

Taxi   Taxi Alba 02 98 89 40 12 Argenton
JP Taxi 02 98 04 30 35 Lanildut
Allo Gwen Taxi 02 98 89 07 85 Le Conquet

Ferries Penn ar Bed (ferries from Le Conquet to Molène, Ouessant, Île de Sein) 02 98 80 80 80 www.pennarbed.fr

OTHER WALKS

Circuit of 12kms along the estuary near Brélès, including menhirs and a château.

Circuit of 12kms around the port of Le Conquet and the Kermorvan peninsula.

For full details, see *Walking and other Activities in Finistere*

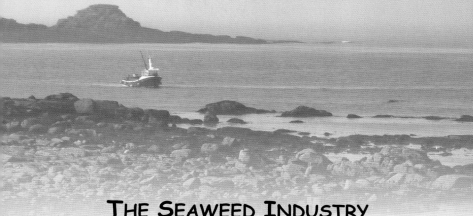

THE SEAWEED INDUSTRY

Seaweed (goémon/algues) has been used by coastal and country dwellers throughout history for fuel, fodder and fertiliser. There are more than 600 varieties in Brittany and modern usage has expanded to include the chemical and the culinary. Medicines, cosmetics and many foodstuffs (additives E401-7, for example) contain seaweed.

A traditional industry in north Finistère in particular, the collection and transport of seaweed once involved thousands of workers and hundreds of boats. In 1999 there remained no more than 62 working boats in Brittany.

The collection season runs from May to October, with goémon de fond (of the laminaires family) gathered from the sea-bed by boat, these days using a hydraulic arm, the scoubidou, rather than a long-armed sickle with guillotine blade. In earlier times the harvest would then be loaded onto horses and carts, a role performed today by tractors and lorries, for transport to factories.

Other types of growing seaweed can be collected on foot at low tide, being cut with a special hand sickle, whilst that thrown up on the beaches by wind and storm can be raked up. It is quite common when coastal walking to see people collecting up bag or trailer loads of seaweed for use on the garden. One less welcome form of seaweed, the bright green ulva lactuca, is such a prolific breeder that many flat coves with little current become scarred with a thick glaucous ring. This sea lettuce, not much used in France, is edible, but gives off an unpleasant sulphurous smell when rotting in mass.

Originally the seaweed was dried in stacks on the sand dunes for 3-4 days and then burnt in ovens – long, thin stone-lined holes in the ground – releasing a yellow, salty smoke over the coastline. This process took a day, and dividers in the oven meant that the compacted result could then be lifted out in blocks of sodium carbonate – 'pain de soude'. This was used in the manufacture of glass, paper and soap, although extract from marine salt eventually replaced it.

The collection of seaweed, practised over many centuries, acquired increased importance after an accidental discovery in 1811. Bernard Courtois had been using seaweed ashes (to economise on wood) in the making of gun-powder, and added too much sulphuric acid to dispose of the waste, releasing a purple vapour. Further investigation by his fellow-scientists led to the classification of a new element, iodine. (The name comes from the Greek iodes = violet.) Iodine came to be used in many processes, from early photography to making glass and paper to the treatment of water and manufacture of pharmaceuticals. 5-6 tons of fresh seaweed produced one ton of dried which in turn reduced to 200kgs of soda. From this amount about 2-3kgs of iodine would result.

The first factory for treating seaweed and extracting iodine was established by François Tissier at Le Conquet in 1829 and many others followed, at Portsall, for example, where the Caroff factory was one of the longest-lasting, at Aber W'rach and Audierne (1874). By 1921 Finistere had a total of 15. There was a decline in this practice after the 1950s, however, when cheap Chilean imports of iodine became available on the free market.

To learn more about the history and traditional way of life of the goémoniers, visit the Maison de l'Algue at Lanildut (see p.71) or the Musée des Goémoniers et de l'Algue at Plouguerneau (see p.50), where a grand Fête des Goémoniers, with costumed demonstrations, is held in August each year.

6. Pointe St-Mathieu - Pont Albert Louppe
Along the Rade de Brest

41 kms

The route begins in a landscape of spectacular craggy heights and striking rock structures around the outstanding site of Pointe St-Mathieu, with its ancient ruined abbey on the wild cliff-top. Together with the city of Brest further along the coast, there is a wide variety of historical interest here including a whole series of forts and lighthouses, and the redoubtable Château of Brest, now housing a maritime museum. The extent and variety of fortifications in this area is my pervading impression of the coast here. Views across the Goulet to the Crozon peninsula also provide a focus for envisaging defensive strategy through the ages for the Rade de Brest, an impressive inland sea with 270kms of heavily indented shoreline.

The route also passes plenty of sandy beaches, an unusual public park, the famous attraction of Oceanopolis and the lively pleasure port of Moulin Blanc.

DIRECTIONS

17/1 Near road bear **R** downhill, round cove along top of beach, then up steps • Stay to **R** of large 🅿 and **CA** on narrow path, followed by wide grassy path round final headland, then up steps to memorial

This sculpture of a grieving Breton woman by Réné Quillivic was first set up in 1927 to commemorate the sailors of WW1. It is now dedicated to all those who have lost their lives at sea in the struggle for liberty over generations.

The nearby artillery battery originates from the time of Louis XV (1710-1774) and was also used in many subsequent conflicts. The 95mm guns emplaced here date from 1888.

• Go **ahead** past memorial, round cove and up to abbey (or fork **L** through 🅿 to hotel, which has bar & restaurant) • Bear **R** round cliffs **(From here there are views to the Tas de Pois - see p.118 - the Cap de la Chèvre and the Pointe du Raz)**

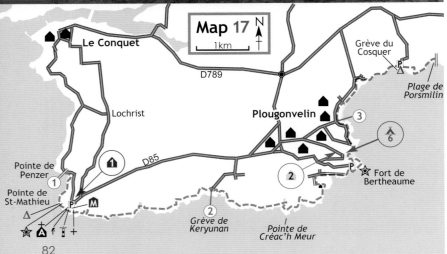

ST MATHIEU

The Benedictine Abbey here was founded in the 11th century, when, according to legend, Breton sailors brought back relics of Saint Matthew from Ethiopia. The ruins today preserve architectural features from early Romanesque to Gothic, including a single wall of the monks' dorter, where each cell had a window on the sea. The lower half of the fire tower kept alight by the monks still stands below the lighthouse that now performs the same function.

In the 17th century Benedictine reforms were imposed and the Congregation of Saint Maur took over the abbey to re-establish the old values of monastic life. A separate building for domestic services was constructed at this time: its underground wine-cellar is still accessible. Abandoned and sold at the time of the Revolution, the

abbey was used as a source of stone for local building projects and left in ruins. Nearby is the parish church, Notre-Dame de Grâce, which retains a 14th century porch.

A small museum about the history and legends of the site nearby is open every day in high season.

From this headland on a clear day the islands of Ouessant (25kms) and Molène (15kms) are visible. Grey seals and bottle-nosed dolphins are sometimes to be seen in the Mer d'Iroise.

• **CA** round cove past abbey, bearing **R** on path • Rejoin track, then bear **R** again on path (**Fortifications soon visible ahead**) • Keep ahead on easy-to-follow path along south coast, passing look-out post, ignoring paths off to **L** (**The numerous WWII bunkers and look-out posts along here testify to the importance of defending Brest**) • Go down steps past little lake, then up again to continue along cliff,

MUR ATLANTIQUE

As part of the 'Atlantic Wall' defensive system the Germans endeavoured to make the coasts of Brittany impregnable by a series of concrete bunkers, anti-aircraft batteries and machine gun posts. Storage areas for water and munitions were often sunk underground, whilst other manned posts were camouflaged against aerial attack. The remaining concrete pillboxes are mostly adorned with bright graffiti these days, although one in a fine state of repair near the Fort de Bertheaume is now in service as a public toilet.

passing seamark (for ships at sea) • Carry on round edge of cliffs, keeping **R** round head of coves (with all the ups and downs)

17/2 At road with access to beach (Grève de Keryunan), cross straight over and continue up steps • Follow hairpin path up very steep hill to Pointe de Keryunan • At fork, go **R**, then keep **ahead** up and down steps and past lake at Poull an Dour • After Pointe Creac'h Meur, go **R** at fork and again at further forks • **Fort of Bertheaume soon comes into view ahead** • After house on left, follow path inland. uphill, staying on same track • At top, go **R** • At end of track, turn **R** along road • At junction go

FORT DE BERTHEAUME

There was a château here as early as 1474. Vauban saw its potential as a key point in defence of the Rade de Brest and fortified the island – accessible at low tide - in 1689. Early methods of access included the 'flying boat', a cradle suspended from a rope and winched across.

The guns from the fort worked in tandem with those across the water at Camaret – a strategic concept which proved its worth in 1694 when a combined Anglo-Dutch attack failed (see p.116).

In 1804, Napoleon wrote angrily to his commander here, ordering him to get out into the straits and engage the English fleet that was blocking the entrance. A series of excuses followed, and even the Dictator gloomily came to the conclusion that a successful outcome was unlikely.

The barracks, underground powder store and lower battery which can be seen today are from a later date. The island was used by the Germans in WWII and surrendered to American troops in September 1944.

ahead on no-through-road • **CA** on track, over bridge, then **ahead** past fort • Bear **R** down little road, then straight over beach at bottom • On other side climb steps and go **R** at top • Follow path to road, there bear **R ahead** • At bottom of road bear **R**

17/3 **CA** on road along front, past TO (or walk along the beach of Trez Hir - 'Long Beach') • 250m turn **R**, then **L** along promenade above beach • At road follow ahead uphill • 200m turn **R** • At mini-roundabout go **R** downhill • Follow **L**, then **CA** on footpath down to coast • Go down steps at end and **CA** • 700m go straight across bottom of P **There is a memorial in the car-park to resistance martyrs** • Go ahead up narrow road, becoming track, parallel with coast • 200m at junction with path, turn **R** • Go ahead up steps and **CA** • After coming down off cliffs, go along top of beach to Porsmilin

18/1 **CA** on cliff path 400m to next beach, Plage de Portez (restaurant/bar) • Follow path parallel with road above beach • At very large P, go diagonally across, then up road (another café/restaurant here by the beach) • Follow road 750m turn **R** • At turning area at end of road go **R** onto coast path • Follow out over wild cliffs • Keep ahead on main path 1.5km • At track go **R**, 50m **R** again onto coast path, dropping steeply • Just before rock formation turn **L** on path downhill

18/2 Follow **R** round deep inlet and **CA** on cliff path • At road, cross it and go back up steps again for a steep climb • At ruined **Fort de Toulbroc'h**, turn **L** to follow green path round behind overgrown buildings

Fort Toulbrac'h

• At another path, turn **L** through barrier, follow track **R, CA** on road • 50m go **R** downhill with views of fort • At bottom of road, bear **L,** then immediately **R** along no-through-road • 50m, bear **R** down green path • Follow **L** over bridge and ahead up steps • Keep ahead on cliff path with steps up and down • By 🅿, turn **R** down to water, then bear **L ahead** up cliff path • Follow this up to Petite Minou, coming out above fort • Here turn **R** down to 🅿, then **L** to **CA** along cliffs • Follow path 1.3kms through pines, behind

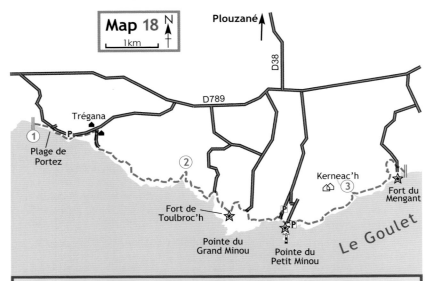

SÉBASTIEN LE PRESTRE DE VAUBAN (1633-1707)

The naval base of Brest has always held a strategic importance for defence and control of Atlantic traffic passing in and out of the Channel. This stretch of coast has a great variety of structures of fortification, from medieval island strongholds to German bunkers. Louis XIV's Royal Engineer Vauban made the most visible contribution with a chain of forts, particularly around the access to the Rade de Brest. His genius lay in selecting sites where defensive works could make use of the terrain and its contours. The overall strategy led to careful correlation of gun emplacements all around the Goulet. See p.96.

MINOU – FORT AND LIGHTHOUSE

Fort du Minou (open weekends 10-7) dates from 1697 and is another link in Vauban's chain of defence for Brest. The lighthouse (1848) forms a directional line with that of Portzic to guide ships along the Goulet. One of the earliest transatlantic cables was laid via the beach here in 1869. It linked Brest with Cape Cod, and the earliest operator of the line was the Anglo-American Telegraph Company.

house, over stream and up steps before turning inland, down to the valley of Kernéac'h

18/3 Cross bridge, then up steep steps onto high cliffs ahead • At highest point and wooden barrier, **CA** to road (**To the right is the Fort du Mengant, where a circular battery protrudes into the sea. Built in 1664 on Vauban's instructions, it had a garrison of 250 men in the mid-18th century and a total of 42 cannon**) • Go **L** along road, 100m turn **R** onto path • At fork go **R** (**this is a lovely chemin creux down through the woods**) • At road go **R**, then down side of Marine Nationale premises • Follow path round to fork, bear **R** uphill

19/1 CA along cliffs over 1km, then follow path down and inland through woodland • At fork soon after, turn **R** downhill • At road, turn **R** downhill (Le Grand Dellec) • Just before beach, go **L** uphill through wooden barrier • Follow path round back of large fort to entrance (**public park**)

FORT DU DELLEC This Vauban installation, with 19th century and WWII additions, has been open to the public as a park and recreational area since the 1980s. It is possible to wander amongst the batteries and barracks, enjoying superb views (on a clear day) from two viewing platforms to the Pointe des Espagnols opposite and the position of other forts in the chain dominating the Goulet.

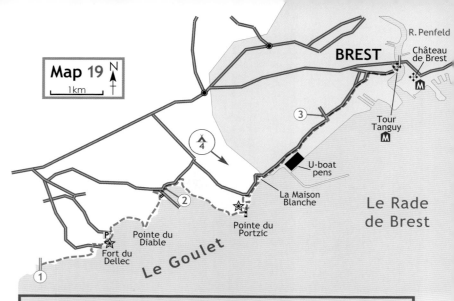

Map 19
N
1km

R. Penfeld

Château
de Brest

BREST

Tour
Tanguy
Ⓜ

Ⓜ

③

4

U-boat
pens

La Maison
Blanche

Le Rade
de Brest

Pointe du
Portzic

P

Pointe du
Diable

Fort du
Dellec

Le Goulet

①

THE GOULET is the narrow channel connecting the Rade de Brest to the Atlantic. It is about 1.8kms wide, and was protected in the 18th century by forts on the north and south (Crozon peninsula) sides. It has been the scene of maritime confrontation over the centuries. Most famously, in 1512, the Cordelière, one of the finest ships of the Breton fleet, was taken unawares near the Pointe de St-Mathieu. Hundreds of guests were aboard, celebrating the feast of St-Laurent, when an English fleet appeared and battle was joined. The Cordelière became involved in a close tussle with The Regent. Grappling irons held the two ships together and hand-to-hand fighting raged for several hours. Finally realising that defeat was inevitable, the Cordelière's captain, Hervé de Portzmoguer, blew up his own ship and took the Regent to the bottom with it.

English blockades of this avenue to the Atlantic were a regular feature of the late 18th and early 19th century, during the War of American Independence and France's Wars of Empire, so much so that it provided the major impetus for the construction of the Nantes/Brest canal, to provide a secure internal supply route across Brittany. The funnel-like effect of this narrow Goulet exacerbates both winds and currents, making headway out into the Atlantic against westerlies very difficult, a fact that aided English blockades of the Rade.

RADE DE BREST

The Rade is an inland sea of 150km², fed by the large rivers Elorn and Aulne, together with many smaller ones, giving a vast catchment area/basin of 2800km². An environmental programme of both preservation and development of the Rade has been in operation for the last ten years, attempting to reconcile the often conflicting needs of the fishing industry, farming and tourism. Water quality is an ongoing issue, with efforts to limit all forms of pollution such as the use of pesticides in agriculture. Altogether the Rade has 270kms of littoral, thanks to many peninsulas and inlets. A lot of this can be walked, but only piecemeal, so the GR34 currently takes an inland route beyond Brest to the crossing of the Aulne near Landévennec.

• From fort entrance, bear **L** along access road 60m, then turn **R** down steps • Follow path round picnic area, at end go straight ahead, finally **R** up steps onto cliff again • Follow path nearest edge, ignoring others • Scramble across last rocky headland (Pointe du Diable accessible to the R) then round to **L** • Follow narrow path up through woods • At track, go **R** on broad lane • At end, follow path **L** and at road turn **R** down to beach (**ALTERNATIVE**: go **R** down very long steep flight of steps, then **L** at bottom to rejoin main route to beach)

19/2 Walk beside beach (where there is a bar/restaurant), then **ahead** up road 600m • Turn **R** where it starts to go uphill, back onto coastal path • Stay on this, ignoring others (**There are many old fortifications here**) • Past large building follow path (former railway), then alongside military enclosure • With Portzic lighthouse just ahead, follow path diverging to **R**, down and round in front of lighthouse • Follow through trees round Fort du Portzic (**From the Pointe du Portzic across to the Pointe des Espagnols, the Goulet is at its narrowest point**) • At road, go **R** • Follow road through little port of Maison Blanche • *CA* on road behind military port of Brest

BREST

Brest was once a stronghold of the Celtic Osismes tribe and then a Roman castellum. It came into the possession of the Dukes of Brittany in the 13th century via Henri, Comte de Léon, who was in need of money and sold the entire town to Jean I Le Roux. In the Wars of Succession a hundred years later, English forces supporting the claim of Jean de Monfort took Brest and held it for nearly fifty years until Richard II returned it to Brittany in 1397.

Cardinal Richlieu, governor of Brittany from 1626, was the first to develop the potential of the city, making it the military port for the Atlantic seaboard. Vauban, who later planned its defences, described the city as 'a royal port with all the advantages one could desire, and in a way that seemed God took pleasure in the arrangement'.

In the mid-18th century Choquet de Lindu was responsible for the development of the arsenal, with workshops, forges and warehouses stretching along both sides of the Penfeld estuary. Ship-building, fitment and armaments were all important, and from here ships sailed across the Atlantic to seal the Americans' bid for independence from the British with a decisive intervention at Chesapeake Bay in 1781.

In 1750 de Lindu built the bagne (prison), a vast establishment housing hundreds of men who were used as labour in the arsenal. Convicts from here were sent to construct the Grand Tranchée of the Nantes-Brest canal at Glomel in Côtes d'Armor. When the prison was closed a hundred years later the alternative 'punishment' of shipping criminals to the colonies was employed.

Remarkably, the medieval château of Brest, strategically placed above the Penfeld estuary, survived the devastation wrought on the rest of the city by allied bombing in WWII (Brest being a vital German U-boat base). Well worth a visit, one can wander the castle defences (including the Tour Azénor - see p.70) outside, and enjoy the interior of the château alongside exhibits of an interesting maritime museum.

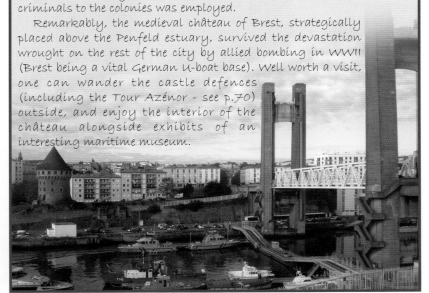

SUBMARINE BASE

Departing British troops destroyed the port installations before the Germans arrived in Brest in June 1940. The first U-boat, U-65, was in the Rade two months later. Construction of the submarine base began in January 1941: in total there were 15 pens - 5 wet (2 berths each) and 10 dry - and the anti-aircraft guns positioned on the roof were soon in action against frequent RAF raids. Little damage was inflicted, however, until the Tallboy bombs were available for use in August 1944 and 15 Lancasters of No.617 Squadron scored six direct hits, shattering the roof. The last U-boat left shortly after this and the Germans surrendered on 21 September.

19/3 1.5kms (at a port entrance), turn **R** uphill, still behind port • **CA** further kilometre • At fork bear **R**, follow 300m to traffic lights, turn **R** (rue de l'église) • Follow downhill to Tour Tanguy • Go up steps to **L** of tower, then **ahead** up to bridge • Turn **R** across bridge

TOUR TANGUY

This (restored) 14th century tower on the west bank of the Penfeld houses a fascinating museum of the history of Brest, including vivid reconstructions by painter and model-maker Jim Sevellec. The document signed by Louis XIV to signal that Brest was to replace Saint-Renan as regional capital in 1681 is also on display here.

20/1 Over bridge turn **R** immediately towards château • At château entrance (on R), cross road towards sculpture at start of promenade opposite • Go to very end of Course Dajot (about 600m), over pedestrian crossing and bear **R** along road • 200m turn **R** (rue Poullic al Lor) • 150m go **L** up steps • At station turn **R** (ignore balisage) to viewpoint and **CA** along footpath • At end turn **L**, up over railway • Far end of bridge turn **R** • Where road splits go up over bridge • On far side turn **R** towards château (school) • Before railway, turn **L** along very narrow footpath

COURSE DAJOT

This 600m promenade was built by convicts from the naval prison in 1769 and extended later to provide a panoramic view over the Rade. Two marble statues designed for the garden are now in the Louvre in Paris, having taken ill to the salty air of Brest!

The tall tower on the southern side is the monument to the American naval forces of WWI, when Brest was an important strategic base. Erected in 1927, it was destroyed by the Germans in 1941 and rebuilt in the same form in 1958.

20/2 At end, go **R** • Follow road 90° **L**, then take first **R** (rue de Guernevez) • Follow this road 90° **L**, to junction, turn **R** (rue Estienne d'Orves) • 400m turn **R** (rue Gounod – **not** the one just before it) • Follow round bend and past ℗ turn sharp **R** (direction Dour Braz) through wooden barrier • Follow path to view point, then **CA** along road • At junction turn **R** downhill • Go under bridge, then turn **L** opposite chapel (rue de Vieux Kerveguen) • Follow **ahead** 400m to just past level crossing (on **L**) and turn **R** • 50m bear **L** and cross railway (with care) • Go under motorway, cross road, then go **ahead** (Chemin de Mezenes)

20/3 At **TJ** of paths go **L** • Keep **ahead** on broad path (roundabout to right) • At road go **L**, then skirt Oceanopolis site and **CA** to Port du Moulin Blanc • Make for promenade by water and follow this to end

OCEANOPOLIS

This vast domed structure contains one of the most popular visitor attractions in Brittany. Polar, tropical and temperate zones include all manner of extraordinarily shaped, sized and coloured examples of ocean life. The popular penguins, sharks and seals seem almost commonplace beside some of the other inhabitants! The site provides an amazingly varied educational and entertaining experience – allow a day to make the most of it.

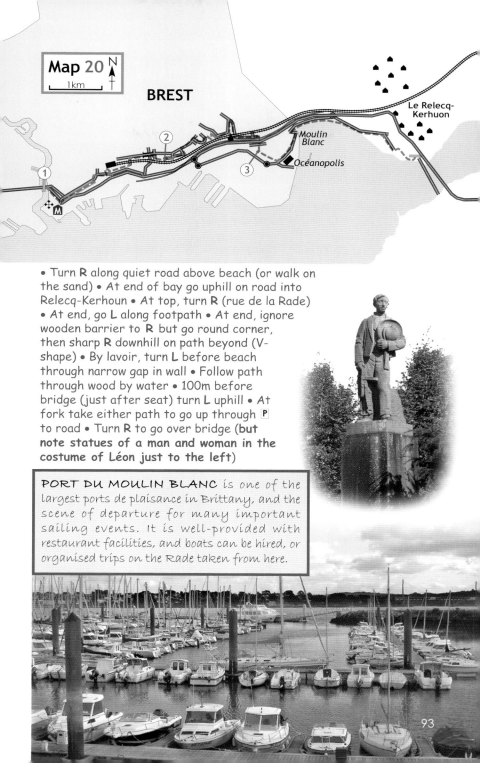

Map 20 N
BREST

Le Relecq-Kerhuon

Moulin Blanc

Océanopolis

• Turn **R** along quiet road above beach (or walk on the sand) • At end of bay go uphill on road into Relecq-Kerhoun • At top, turn **R** (rue de la Rade) • At end, go **L** along footpath • At end, ignore wooden barrier to **R** but go round corner, then sharp **R** downhill on path beyond (V-shape) • By lavoir, turn **L** before beach through narrow gap in wall • Follow path through wood by water • 100m before bridge (just after seat) turn **L** uphill • At fork take either path to go up through P to road • Turn **R** to go over bridge (**but note statues of a man and woman in the costume of Léon just to the left**)

PORT DU MOULIN BLANC is one of the largest ports de plaisance in Brittany, and the scene of departure for many important sailing events. It is well-provided with restaurant facilities, and boats can be hired, or organised trips on the Rade taken from here.

6. PRACTICAL INFORMATION

SHOPS & SERVICES
- **Plougonvelin** TO (internet point) 02 98 48 30 18
  www.plougonvelin-fr.com Mkt Sun am
- **Brest** TO 02 98 44 24 96 www.brest-metropole-tourisme.fr

ACCOMMODATION
Hotel
1. Hostellerie de la Point St-Mathieu (on route) 29217 Plougonvelin
   02 98 89 00 19 www.pointe-saint-mathieu.com
Chambres d'hôte
2. Brigitte Le Mouillour (100m) 53 rue de Perzel, 29217 Plougonvelin
   02 98 38 00 29 brigittelemouillour@wanadoo.fr
Camping
3. Camping les Terrasses de Bertheaume (on route) Route de Perzel,
   29217 Plougonvelin 02 98 48 32 37 www.camping-brest.com
   Open all year
4. Camping du Goulet (1km) Sainte Anne du Portzic, 29200 Brest
   02 98 45 86 86 www.campingdugoulet.com Open all year

TRANSPORT
Brest airport (at Guipavas) Flights to and from Birmingham, Exeter,
   Southampton, Manchester, Luton. www.airport.cci-brest.fr
   Shuttle bus to centre of Brest
Brest railway station - train links (e.g. Morlaix, Paris) www.sncf.com
Brest buses www.bibus.fr
Brest - ferries to Ouessant and Molène   www.pennarbed.fr
Boat trips on the Rade www.Azénor.com

OTHER WALKS

Brest TO has a series of excellent leaflets *Balades Urbaines* covering the
most interesting parts of the city, with good maps, illustrations, history
and an emphasis on architectural details.

FORTIFICATIONS

Walking the coast will soon produce an awareness of the variety of methods of defence and fortification man has employed over the centuries in this part of Brittany with its Atlantic shore and proximity to the entrance of the Channel.

The éperon barré or fortified spur of land jutting out into the sea was used in the Iron Age (c500BC) as a defensive measure against attack by land and sea. A series of banks and ditches running across the neck of the peninsula, with only a single narrow access point, was relatively easy to defend against numbers. Inside, natural rock formations at the points were employed as look-out stations or further layers of protection. Rain water, driven by the west wind, was carefully guarded in suitable hollows. Archaeological excavation has shown that many temporary dwelling places lay within the fortifications so that an entire community could shelter within in times of danger. At Castelmeur on Cap Sizun, for example, there is evidence that 95 huts once crowded on the peninsula for protection. Other good examples can be seen at Beg Monom and Lostmarc'h.

During the later stages of Roman occupation of Brittany, the so-called litus saxonicum (Saxon shore) referred to a series of coastal fortifications, on both sides of the channel, which were used throughout the Dark Ages and later became the mottes and keeps of the earliest châteaux. These are often on estuaries which allowed access to the interior, such as the Guillec (château of Kerouzéré) and Penzé (ruins of Château de Penhoat) near Morlaix.

As seafaring and trade developed. together with the nation states of England and France, defence of the coasts became an organised business against the threat of attack and invasion. Despite Brittany's independent status until 1532, the coast was a frequent target for English corsairs in search of booty or in retaliation for raids by their Breton counterparts. After a surprise English attack that destroyed much of the town of Morlaix in 1522, it was decided to invest in a permanent fortification utilising a large rock at the mouth of the Morlaix river. In 1544 the Château du Taureau was thus established and exercised a powerful deterrent against future incursions.

Château du Taureau

Fort Bertheaume

In fact, English and Dutch ships posed a fairly constant threat to Brittany during the 15-19th centuries as political, colonial and trade interests conflicted. A series of look-out posts and guard-houses lined the coast, later employed by customs' agents in pursuit of smugglers, and defences were further strengthened by new forts constructed in the 1860s under Napoleon III.

At the end of the 17th century, Louis XIV's chief engineer Sébastien le Prestre de Vauban conceived a systematic series of forts and batteries to counter the threat of the British navy. His priority was defence of Brest, positioned on the superb natural harbour, almost an inland sea, of the Rade de Brest. A day's walk from the Pointe St-Mathieu to Brest will take in five major sites at Bertheaume, Minou, Mengant, Dellec and Portzic. These Vauban forts continued to be utilised in subsequent centuries with appropriate up-dating of guns and equipment. At Fort du Dellec, for example, which is now a public park, significant development took place in the 19th century and the WWII additions can also be explored. Viewing platforms here give an unparalleled view over the Goulet, the narrow entrance to the Rade, which was frequently blockaded by English ships.

On the coastal route in Finistère, remnants of the WWII Atlantic Wall are ubiquitous, and hardly a one has survived without the decoration of colourful modern graffiti. The Germans built concrete structures such as bunkers and batteries prolifically, often using material from the pebble sea-defences of the Baie d'Audierne. (The remains of the factory can still be seen at Croas An Douar - see p.170.)

Offensively, the submarine base at Brest and the operation of U-boats were of crucial importance to their naval strategy, as constant allied air-raids over the city showed. The Goulet was therefore defended by a series of gun-batteries to protect against incursions by sea or air, and such precautionary structures can be seen along the entire coastline, especially where the terrain favoured landings, despite the lack of sufficient man-power to render them constantly active. The Museum of the Battle of the Atlantic, right on the coastal path near Camaret, gives an idea of the grim realities of this deadly struggle for supremacy at sea.

7. Elorn - Aulne
Between two bridges
45 kms

There is no continuous path around the peninsulas between the Elorn and the Aulne rivers, unfortunately, and although many bits are walkable, overall the benefits do not outweigh the frustrations of trying to stay within sight of the water. The GR34 cuts out the many small estuaries of the Rade de Brest and runs inland for much of the way. In fact, this can provide a welcome change from coastal walking given the interesting places and varied countryside it passes. On the other hand the views and atmosphere of this interesting area deserve greater exploration and it is to be hoped that a full coastal path is developed in the future.

If time allows, a couple of exploratory forays of this fine fringe of the Rade are given at the end of this section in summary detail (see p.106-7) - the second is highly recommended, despite the road walking necessary to join up the salient parts. Plans are in hand for linking the Daoulas/Logonna-Daoulas stretches during the course of 2008, so there may soon be a significant improvement on the suggested route .

COQUILLES ST-JACQUES

That most traditional of Breton delicacies, scallops, are important in this part of the Rade. The little port of Tinduff in the commune of Plougastel has a hatchery for fostering the young of this hermaphrodite species, which reproduces through the pink corail containing both sperm and eggs. The larvae are fed on plankton in special tanks for the first three months and then submerged in pots until they reach a size of 30mm, when they are ready to be 'sown' in the Rade in spring or autumn. This method of stocking the deeper waters more than doubled the yield during the 1990s.

The recovery of productive levels of coquilles St-Jacques has been the symbolic aim of the project 'Contrat de Baie', a long-standing environmental scheme to combat pollution in the bay, promoting an integrated management of water in the estuaries and throughout the watershed of the Rade de Brest, an area of 2800km², reaching as far east as Cotes d'Armor.

BRIDGES

The Pont Albert Louppe was built in the 1920s across the Elorn estuary to improve connections with Brest. During WWII the Germans destroyed one arch to hamper Allied progress, but the bridge was reopened in 1949. Increasing traffic over succeeding decades led to the construction of the Pont d'Iroise just beside it in the early 90s.

Although the Elorn is the boundary between Leon and Cornouaille (Kerne in Breton), there is a Breton saying: Etre Landerne hag ar Faou n'emeur nag e Leon nag e Kerne (Between Landerneau and Le Faou, one is neither in Leon, nor in Cornouaille). At each end of the old bridge stand two representative statues, one male and one female, dressed in the traditional costumes of their respective territories.

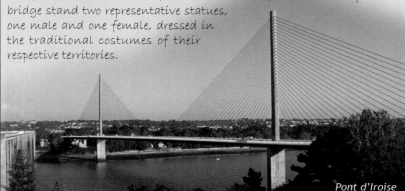

Pont d'Iroise

PLOUGASTEL-DAOULAS

Early economic wealth here came through the production of linen and hemp, those staples of the region. In 1766 the engineer and botanist Amédée-François Frézier brought the strawberry to Plougastel. Now famous for this product, the town has a museum dedicated to their history and a Fêtes des Fraises. See www.musee-fraise.net

There was originally an ancient priory of the abbey at Daoulas on the site of the current church. This neo-gothic late 19th century

structure by Le Bigot was badly damaged during WWII and then restored in 1951. The beams of the nave are painted in the colours of Plougastel's traditional costume.

American shelling also destroyed many statues on the exceptional calvaire outside the church, and one US officer, John Skilton, raised money on his return home to aid the restoration funds. 182 figures in Kersanton granite adorn a base of Logonna stone, both these being local materials. The calvaire (1598-1604) was an ex-voto offering after an outbreak of the plague.

DIRECTIONS (see map on next page)

21/1 Go **L** to see statues; **R** to cross Elorn. **Views of Brest and its Rade to right, river valley to left leading to fringes of Monts d'Arrée where it rises. Pass other pair of statues on Cornouaille side; fountain beyond with inscription "Iec'hed Mad" (good health) – but don't drink the water.** Picnic tables and public toilets here. • Go **ahead** to roundabout, take exit opposite, bearing **R** uphill • 40m turn **R** • 110m turn **L** on footpath uphill • In hamlet, turn **L** immediately on footpath to follow main route [**or turn R to follow Option 1** - see p.106] • *CA* 1km, swinging **R** at junction of paths; **R** again at fork

21/2 At road turn **L** • **Ahead** at crossroads towards Plougastel-Daoulas • Bear **R** towards church • Go **R**

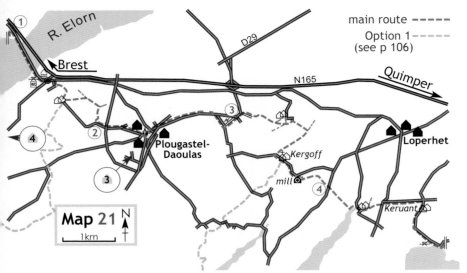

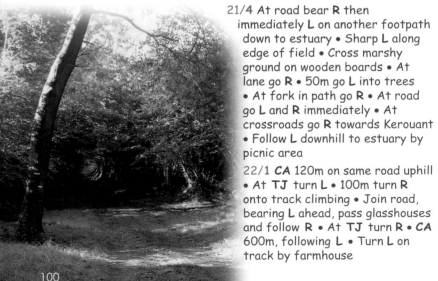

of church to see calvaire • **Ahead** from calvaire, cross open space (market place) • *CA* on rue Francis Guivarch • *CA* at junction by stone cross (signed *toutes directions*) 1km • After **R** bend, go **L** on track just beyond electricity station

21/3 At road, bear **R** ahead 20m • Bear **R** down another track, keep ahead, ignore other paths • Near hamlet, turn **R**, then **R** again at junction of paths • Enter Kergoff past manor house and its chapel • Turn **L** at **TJ** • [125m on **R**, **Option 1 rejoins**] • *CA* 500m, passing mill and pond • Climbing again 100m, turn **R** onto track • Follow 90° **L**

21/4 At road bear **R** then immediately **L** on another footpath down to estuary • Sharp **L** along edge of field • Cross marshy ground on wooden boards • At lane go **R** • 50m go **L** into trees • At fork in path go **R** • At road go **L** and **R** immediately • At crossroads go **R** towards Kerouant • Follow **L** downhill to estuary by picnic area

22/1 *CA* 120m on same road uphill • At **TJ** turn **L** • 100m turn **R** onto track climbing • Join road, bearing **L** ahead, pass glasshouses and follow **R** • At **TJ** turn **R** • *CA* 600m, following **L** • Turn **L** on track by farmhouse

22/2 At road go **R** uphill • At junction bear **R** • *CA* same road passing *Croas Guénolé* • Don't follow R, go **ahead** uphill to Daoulas Abbey • *CA* down narrow road **R** of abbey (see below) • At bottom follow rue du Pont **R**, cross branch of river • At junction bear **R** (signed to mairie) • Follow same road beside estuary • 800m **Option 2 leaves by coastal path on R** (see p.107) • Otherwise, *CA* uphill 150m, turn **L** • 80m turn **R** onto track, then immediately **L** onto footpath • At top of *chemin creux* bear **R** slightly downhill

22/3 At main road turn **R** • 30m turn **L** up track • At cross-tracks at top of hill, go **ahead** past stone cross (intermittent views back to Rade de Brest) • *CA* on road to **TJ**, turn **L** • 275m turn **R** opposite cross • *CA* same road 3kms to L'Hôpital-Camfrout (**with good views of Monts d'Arrée to left, Ménez Hom to right and Forêt du Gars across motorway. Picnic table near river, just past mill in Wood of**

DAOULAS

The name of this little town, from the Breton *daou* and *(g)las*, means two rivers. Its port on the Mignonne saw the export of cloth to Portugal, England and Holland. Later industrial development included the manufacture of porcelain. The château here was destroyed by the English in 1472 and not rebuilt.

Daoulas is most famous for the Abbey, founded in the 12th century by the viscount of Léon. The church today owes much to later restoration, with some of the original nave intact. Unique in Finistere is the exceptional and delicate cloister behind the abbey, where a monolithic medieval basin still stands. The abbey park is a restful place to while away a couple of hours with its oratory, fontaine and renowned medieval-style medicinal gardens, instrumental in modern scientific research, and containing healing plants from all over the world. There is also a large cultural centre, which regularly houses major ethnic exhibitions, and contains a café and shop.

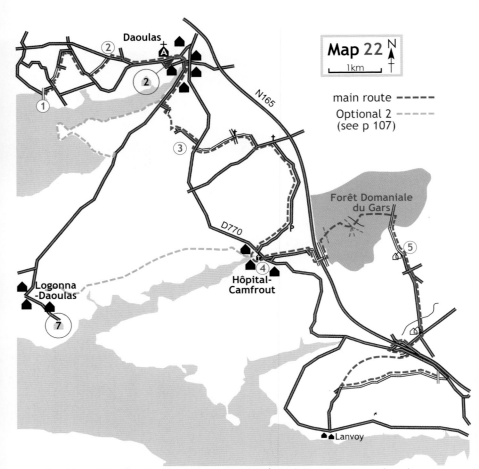

Map 22

main route -----
Optional 2 ----
(see p 107)

Daoulas

N165

Forêt Domaniale
du Gars

D770

P

Hôpital-
Camfrout

Logonna
-Daoulas

Lanvoy

the Hermitage) • Cross main road in L'Hôpital Camfrout, go ahead past telephone box, [**Option 2 rejoins**] bear **L** over pedestrian bridge • Go up to **R** of church

22/4 100m turn **L** • At junction go **ahead** on one-way street • **CA** 550m, bearing **L** in **P** past **memorial to wars in Indo-China and Korea** • **CA** up narrow lane (**The tiny hermitage of St-Conval is in the** **grounds of a house 800m to** **the left here**) • Don't follow lane R, go **ahead** up stony track • Follow **R** parallel with motorway • 130m turn **L** over bridge and **L** on other side • 250m turn **R** into forest • At cross-paths go **ahead** • **CA** on same path uphill and bending **R**

102

HOPITAL CAMFROUT

This was the site of an 11th century priory which provided shelter for pilgrims on their way to Landévennec or Compostella. It was later taken over by the Hospitaliers de St-Jean. The name is from the Breton cam (crooked) and frout (stream). The building situated on rocks just south of the church (passed on the route) housed lepers in the 17th century.

- Go ahead to **L** of picnic table at junction
- Cross stream, up again and **ahead** through clearing • Through wooden barrier, turn **R** onto rough road

22/5 At hamlet **CA** on road • Go **ahead** at crossroads • 130m fork **R** onto old Roman road • At junction bear **R** downhill • At **TJ** turn **R** • Follow under motorway • Turn **L** just after • 200m turn **R** up track (the main road is a short-cut but unsafe and unpleasant walking) • At top of track **CA** along edge of field, then *chemin creux*, climbing slowly • At multi-junction, turn **L** on rough track

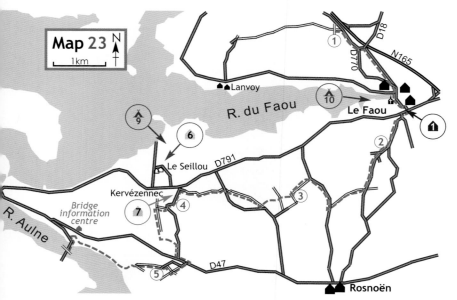

Map 23

23/1 At road (garage and motorway ahead) turn **R** along D770 (**care needed, busy road**) • At multiple junction bear **L** uphill (D18) • 50m turn **R** • 1km bear **L** onto main road into Le Faou • Cross bridge over estuary, pass church, go up main street • At top of street, bear **L** past little market square • Continue **R** side of larger square • At junction (signed Crozon) turn **R** • Soon after bear **L**, then immediately fork **R** (signed Rosnoën) • **CA** on this road out into country

LE FAOU

There was once a thriving port here shipping oak and beech from the nearby Forêt de Cranou to the shipyards at Brest. 'Faou' is the Breton for beech.

The attractive gothic-style church of St-Saveur with its recently restored bell-tower (dating from 1628) dominates the estuary. Niched statues of the twelve apostles in the south porch are on view even when the church is closed.

The main street of Le Faou retains many 16th century houses, their ground floors built of local stone from Logonna with the darker Kersanton granite framing doors and windows. The corbelled upper storey and attic levels were originally of pan de bois construction (half-timbered & cob): the slate cladding is a later addition from a time when wooden houses were regarded as an unacceptable fire risk.

23/2 650m turn **R** (signed La Trest) • At fork go **L** (**views back to Le Faou, estuary entering Rade, and Monts d'Arrée**) • 800m at top of rise turn **R** down track • At road turn **R** downhill • 600m turn **L** up track opposite farm

23/3 Near top of track by green board turn **R** into trees • At top cross track, slightly **L**, and ahead along edge of field (metal sign with red arrow) • Follow field boundary **L** • At end, turn **R** on track downhill • At road, cross and go **ahead** along track • *CA* on access road to junction, turn **L** (**Rando-plume Kervézennec here**)

23/4 *CA* 500m uphill, following **R** and **L**, then turn **R** along track • 250m turn **L** at **TJ** of tracks • At top go **ahead** into wood • Down steep path, turning **L** to follow up stream • At road turn **R** 400m to **TJ** • Turn **L** along main road • 100m turn **R** • At **R** bend go **ahead** along track • At cross-paths go **R** • At road go **L**

23/5 100m bear **R** along track downhill • Don't follow sharp **L** (**views of estuary ahead**) but turn **R** • Follow path round head of valley • Approaching Aulne estuary, *CA* high above the water • Follow path, climbing above suspension bridge (Pont de Térénez), to junction of tracks, turn **L** downhill • At road turn **L** to bridge across the Aulne

NB A new bridge is currently being constructed here for opening in 2009/10. Building work may effect access: be alert for re-routing signs. An exhibition centre about the new bridge is open every afternoon (on the Rosnoën road).

Option 1 – Plougastel peninsula

A 45km circuit (yellow signage) covers the Presqu'île de Plougastel, although not very much is directly by the water. It will, however, provide some stunning views of the white urban mass of Brest glinting across a vast expanse of blue often dotted with boats and yachts. The strategic defensive positions of the Rade are put into context by a good look from the height of the Pointe de Caro (this being the best panoramic view, as the Pointe d'Armorique is a military site and therefore off-limits). A leaflet about this circuit is available from the tourist office in the centre of Plougastel.

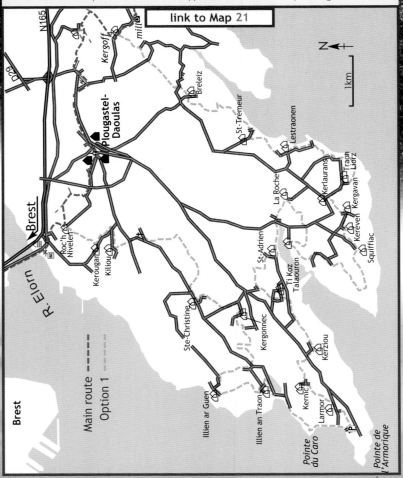

link to Map **21**

N165

D29

Kergoff

mill

Breleiz

Plougastel-Daoulas

St-Tremeur

Lestraonen

La Roche

Kerlaurans

Traon Liorz

Kergavan

Kereven

Squiffiac

Brest

R. Elorn

Roc'h Nivelen

Kerougard

Kiliou

St-Adrien

Ti Koz Talaouron

Ste-Christine

Kergonnec

Kerziou

Illien ar Guen

Illien an Traon

Kernic

Larmor

Pointe du Caro

Pointe de l'Armorique

1km

Brest

Main route

Option 1

Option 2 – Daoulas peninsula

From Daoulas it is possible to walk by the estuary and then along the wooded hillside just above the water to continue around the Pointe de Rosmélec, a most enjoyable route. This is in fact part of a circuit, but turning right instead along the main road towards Logonna-Daoulas and then right again (towards Kerliver and Le Quinquis) enables a connection (after 5kms) with the sentier côtier around the Anse du Roz and Grève de Yelen before reaching the very attractive Pointe du Bindy, with its shingly beaches and two adjacent islands. From here the coastal path, skirting the Anse du Bourg, runs all the way to Moulin Mer, from which it is a fairly short walk into Logonna-Daoulas, where there is a shop and refreshments. It would then be possible to walk along the road to Hôpital-Camfrout (4kms) and rejoin the route given in this section.

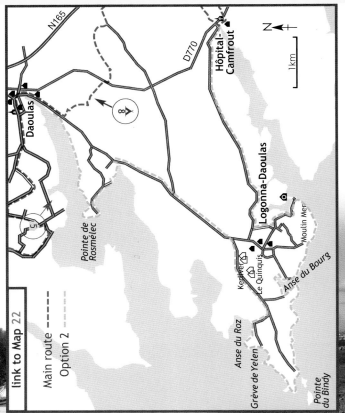

7. PRACTICAL INFORMATION

SHOPS & SERVICES
- **Plougastel-Daoulas** TO open all year 02 98 40 34 98 Mkt Thurs
- **Daoulas** TO 02 98 21 37 67 www.tourisme-landerneau-daoulas.fr
  Mkt Sun am
- **L'Hopital-Camfrout**
- **Le Faou** TO 02 98 81 06 85

ACCOMMODATION
Hotels
1. Hôtel de Beauvoir (on route) 11 Place aux Foires, 29590 Le Faou
   02 98 81 90 31 www.hotel-beauvoir.com
Chambres d'hôte
2. Ar Baradoz Bihan (on route) 12 rue de l'Eglise, 29460 Daoulas
   02 98 85 04 87 www.membres.lycos.fr/baradozbihan
Chambres chez l'habitant
3. M & Mme Bihan (600m) 29 rue du Printemps, 29470 Plougastel-Daoulas
4. M & Mme Kervella (1.5km/Option 1) 185 Route de Prat Bihan,
   Traouidan, 29470 Plougastel-Daoulas 02 98 40 68 80
5. Domaine Moulin Mer (6kms/Option 2 on route) route de Moulin Mer,
   29460 Logonna-Daoulas 02 98 07 24 45
   www.domaine-moulin-mer.com
6. La Ferme Auberge (1km) Le Seillou, 29590 Rosnoën 02 98 81 92 14
Rando-Plume
7. Martine et Joël Le Guirriec (on route) Kervézennec, 29590 Rosnoën
   02 98 81 93 84 http://perso.orange.fr/gite-ty-bihan
Camping
8. Camping de Gouelet Ker (on route of Option 2) 29460 Logonna-Daoulas
   02 98 81 06 85 Open all year
9. Camping du Seillou (1km) Le Seillou, 29590 Rosnoën 02 98 81 92 14
10. Municipal camping (500m) rue de la Grève, 29590 Le Faou
    02 98 81 90 44 (mairie) Open June to September

TRANSPORT
Bus: for (infrequent) service Brest - Le Faou, see www.viaoo29.fr
Taxi: Jean-Yves Cosquer 02 98 04 23 20 Plougastel-Daoulas
       Taxis Thierry 02 98 07 003 11 Lopheret

OTHER WALKS
A 9km circuit around Plougastel-Daoulas starts at Port du Caro and
includes the Pointe du Corbeau.
An 11km chapels circuit starts from La Fontaine Blanche just outside
Plougastel.

8. Pont de Térénez - l'Aber

The Crozon Peninsula

85 kms

The Crozon peninsula offers the most sensational walking in Brittany: vast sandy beaches, the dizzying splendour of high cliffs, an abundance of coves filled with calm turquoise water or crashing waves according to the time and season, and spectacular panoramic views of land and sea unfolding with every step. Much of the time the coastal path is well-away from habitations, particularly in the southern extension of the peninsula towards Cap de la Chèvre, giving an atmospheric sense of wild land unchanged over many centuries.

It is also an area rich in varied human monuments, however, including unusual prehistoric remains in the form of the Lagatjar alignments, a remarkable ruined abbey at Landévennec and an elaborate 20th tribute to the bravery of men in war-time at Pen-hir. The ubiquitous coastal fortifications have also left their mark: the éperon barré (c500BC) at Lostmarc'h should be singled out for mention, together with the glowing ochre brick of the Tour Vauban from an age when English attacks were commonplace around these shores. Much land on the northern coast is still under military control (and therefore inaccessible), with a naval air base at Lanvéoc and submarine station on Île Longue.

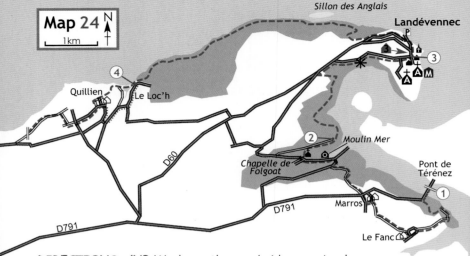

DIRECTIONS (NB Works on the new bridge may involve some re-routing. Be prepared for diversions)

24/1 Over bridge, turn **L** behind compound fence • Follow path 750m, first uphill, then **L** down to water • At bottom turn **R** • Follow track along estuary then uphill to hamlet of Le Fanc • Bear **L** along road 130m • Turn **R** and fork **L** at once up track • Follow to Marros, going **L** at road • At **TJ** turn **R** to D791 • Cross over and **CA** on track downhill 1.2km, ignoring other paths • At road, go **R** and follow **L** (signed Moulin Mer) • **CA** 650m past Moulin Mer, bearing **R** to Chapelle de Folgoat

CHAPELLE DE FOLGOAT (Fool's Wood) The original chapel on this spot was built in 1645 to commemorate a miracle. Salaun, a simpleton (Fol) who lived in these woods, surviving on bread and water from the brooklet, could say only 'Ave Maria'. When he died and was buried in this idyllic spot, a lily showing the same words sprang up from the grave and was found to be growing from Salaun's mouth. The stained-glass windows of the restored chapel recall the legend. A pardon, or religious celebration including a procession, is held here each Ascension Day.

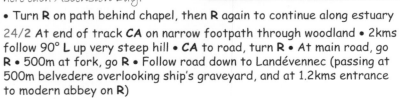

• Turn **R** on path behind chapel, then **R** again to continue along estuary

24/2 At end of track **CA** on narrow footpath through woodland • 2kms follow 90° **L** up very steep hill • **CA** to road, turn **R** • At main road, go **R** • 500m at fork, go **R** • Follow road down to Landévennec (passing at 500m belvedere overlooking ship's graveyard, and at 1.2kms entrance to modern abbey on **R**)

LANDÉVENNEC

Ruins of the ancient abbey and the excellent museum on its site are the highlights of this appealing and tranquil waterside village. St-Guénolé, a pupil of St-Budoc (see p.70), and his eleven followers founded a simple church here in the 6th century. The abbey which developed adopted the Benedictine order in 818, in accordance with the edict of Louis le Pieux for religious establishments in Brittany. It became a renowned centre of learning and study, producing fine illustrated books (shown in the museum) and, of great historical importance, the extraordinarily detailed Cartulaire containing economic and social transactions for all the abbey's widespread holdings.

In 913, marauding Vikings sailed across the Rade and sacked the abbey – archaeological work has revealed that it was burned - although the monks and most treasures probably got away in time. They returned later, and despite further depredations in succeeding centuries of war and upheaval, the abbey continued until dissolution at the time of the Revolution. The ruins were bought by the Comte de Chalus in 1875 for preservation and restoration.

The site returned to the Benedictines in the 1950s and a new abbey was built higher up the hill. This continues the Benedictine tradition with a fine library of books and documents on Breton history. There is also a large shop selling fruit sweets made here by the monks from their rich orchards.

24/3 At bottom of hill (entrance to ancient abbey on R) turn **L** • Walk through village, past church • Before port **P**, follow road **L** uphill 1.3kms • before main road, take footpath on **R** • Follow zig-zags down to shore then **L** through woods above Sillon des Anglais • **CA** 5kms, sometimes near waterline, sometimes climbing to viewpoints • Final descent to Le Loc'h is steep and needs care • At road, go **R** to beach

Le Loc'h

24/4 ALTERNATIVES: EITHER walk down pebbles towards waterline to cross stream to digue • Continue up into woods on narrow path • At **TJ** of paths turn **L**, then follow **R** uphill to hamlet of Quillien • At road go straight ahead 60m, then **L** • After 100m turn **R** on road **OR** continue along road 400m, go **R** at fork, follow 500m then turn **R** and **R** again uphill to Quillien • Here follow road round to **L** and ahead where path comes in from **R** to join this road

• Follow road to **TJ**, go straight over onto track • 80m turn **R** downhill
• At the bottom follow track **L**, then ahead

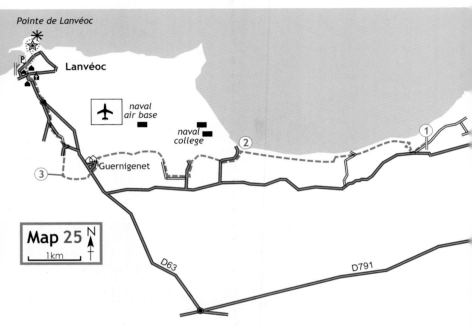

Pointe de Lanvéoc

Lanvéoc

naval
air base

naval
college

Guernigenet

Map 25 N
1km

D63   D791

25/1 CA to road and go **R** • Immediately go **R** again through wooden gate (signed Le Stang 3.7kms) • Follow zig-zag path downhill towards water • Emerging from wood at horseshoe bend in track, cross it and go straight ahead on very narrow path • 300m follow up into woods (**a concessionary path on private property**), then through trees above water • (**The path is fairly clear and there are waymarks at irregular intervals. The naval college can soon be glimpsed ahead**) (An alternative is to bear **R** downhill to the beach and go along it, but it is a very rocky and uncomfortable long walk)

25/2 At entrance to naval college, follow road **L** uphill • 500m turn **R** on narrow path plunging downhill and (muddily) round back of naval premises • At little road, turn **L** uphill • 400m, at crest, go **R** down track along edge of camping/activity site • At junction of paths, go straight on • Follow track **R** downhill, dropping steeply towards wood, then climbing alongside security fence • Where path divides, bear **R** • At grassy clearing bear **R** on uphill • Alongside open field **CA** • In hamlet of Guernigenet, **CA** on road 100m to junction with main D63 • Cross and **CA** on track ahead • 60m bear **L**

25/3 At junction of paths in clearing (**on this pretty wooded route**) turn **R** • At road **CA** • At junction, turn **L** • Past a couple of houses bear **R** and **CA** on track (often very muddy) • **CA** where track becomes access road • At junction, bear **R** and **CA** to roundabout • **CA** to centre bourg • Continue past mairie, bear **L** near church, then **R** at once • **CA** straight over at mini-roundabout, down narrow path between buildings • 200m go down steps, then **R** at road • Turn **L** to Ⓟ, and leave there **L** up steps through hedge

DIVERSION: continue along road to point and then return to Ⓟ.

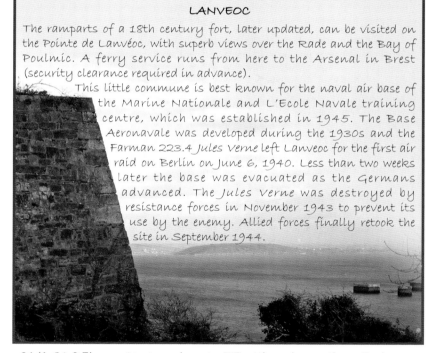

LANVEOC

The ramparts of a 18th century fort, later updated, can be visited on the Pointe de Lanvéoc, with superb views over the Rade and the Bay of Poulmic. A ferry service runs from here to the Arsenal in Brest (security clearance required in advance).

This little commune is best known for the naval air base of the Marine Nationale and L'Ecole Navale training centre, which was established in 1945. The Base Aeronavale was developed during the 1930s and the Farman 223.4 Jules Verne left Lanveoc for the first air raid on Berlin on June 6, 1940. Less than two weeks later the base was evacuated as the Germans advanced. The Jules Verne was destroyed by resistance forces in November 1943 to prevent its use by the enemy. Allied forces finally retook the site in September 1944.

26/1 **CA** 2.5kms • At steps down to **TJ** with sunken path, go **R**, down to beach, then **L** along little green path by shore, soon climbing into woods • Cross bridge and go **ahead**, down steps, then **L** up track • Bear **L** in Ⓟ, then bear **R** uphill on road • At junction just after, ignore track ahead - follow road **R** uphill • Go through hamlet to main road (D55), turn **R** down to causeway

26/2 Walk across causeway, then turn **L** alongside Étang du Fret • **CA** 1200m, then turn **R** (**not when first marked on tree but a bit further, clearly signed**) uphill • 100m at junction of paths turn **L** • At top go **ahead** on reaching a track • At main road (D55b) turn **L** along it • 100m before roundabout, turn **R** on track • At road cross straight over and go ahead (triangle of roads) • 25m turn **L** • At hamlet turn **L** just before tiny cottage (**Camping Pieds dans L'eau is ahead**) • Follow path out of trees and along top of open fields

26/3 Before reaching road, turn **R** downhill • **CA** downhill when track turns into caravan park • At beach, with Île du Renard ahead, turn **L** • Follow top of beach 40m, then bear **L** over bridge into **P** • Go **L** up little road, and at the junction shortly after go **R** (**unremarkable Chapelle de St-Fiacre is 300m to the L here**) • At main road bear **R** along it • Then go **L** and follow little road alongside main one • For next 500m path criss-crosses main road, using old roads running alongside • 75m after second section of old road turn **L** and immediately **R** along old grassy road (ignore no-through-road ahead) • 120m go **L** along no-through-road • At fork bear **R**

26/4 At top where track ends, turn **R** on narrow path • At little road, go **ahead** • At junction turn **R** and immediately fork **L** • **CA** 750m to **TJ** and cross to footpath towards coast (**Camaret is now visible across the water**) • At coast turn **L**, then follow path above beach between hedges • Go straight across **P** (or walk along beach if preferred) and continue up onto gorse covered low cliff • Keep on main path between houses • Past house on **R** with wire fence, turn **R** • Walk along top of pebble beach to next **P**

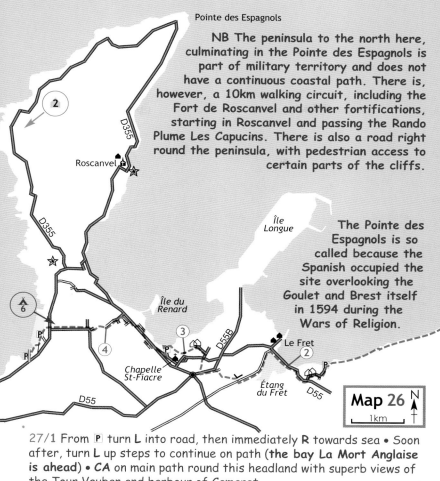

Pointe des Espagnols

NB The peninsula to the north here, culminating in the Pointe des Espagnols is part of military territory and does not have a continuous coastal path. There is, however, a 10km walking circuit, including the Fort de Roscanvel and other fortifications, starting in Roscanvel and passing the Rando Plume Les Capucins. There is also a road right round the peninsula, with pedestrian access to certain parts of the cliffs.

2

D355

Roscanvel

Île Longue

D355

The Pointe des Espagnols is so called because the Spanish occupied the site overlooking the Goulet and Brest itself in 1594 during the Wars of Religion.

6

Île du Renard

3

D55B

Le Fret

2

1

4

P

Chapelle St-Fiacre

Étang du Frêt

D55

P

D55

Map 26 N

1km

27/1 From P turn **L** into road, then immediately **R** towards sea • Soon after, turn **L** up steps to continue on path (**the bay La Mort Anglaise is ahead**) • **CA** on main path round this headland with superb views of the Tour Vauban and harbour of Camaret

LA MORT ANGLAISE On the cliff of La Mort Anglaise, it is possible to see the geological wonder of a beautiful anticline fold in Grès Armoricain (whitish sandstone made of 80% of quartz grains) from the beginning of the Palaeozoic era, around 460 million years ago.

The unusual name of these cliffs derives from an abortive attempt at landing, under heavy fire, by the English fleet during an attack on Camaret in 1694.

La Mort Anglaise

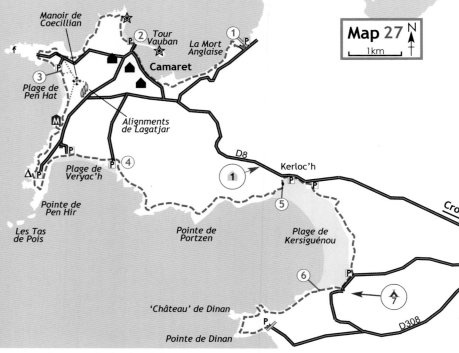

• Where path divides (R to beach) go **L** inland, up steps, then on path between hedges • This finally broadens out and arrives in Camaret, above port • At road bear **R** and go right along front, around harbour

27/2 At end go **R** to see Tour Vauban (open June-Sept) and Chapelle de Rocamadour, or, to continue walk, go **L** through P and ahead

---

CAMARET

This colourful fishing port has the unusual natural feature of a long, curved cob or sillon stretching out into the bay. At the end is the defensive Tour Vauban (1689), which served its purpose in warding off a combined anglo-dutch attack in 1694. A legacy of that event was the loss of the top of the bell-tower of the nearby seafarers' Church of Rocamadour. This stopping point for pilgrims on their way to the shrine in Lot was almost destroyed by fire in 1910 and then accurately restored.

Camaret was also the site of testing for the first submarine, commissioned by Napoleon and designed by the American Robert Fulton in 1801.

Pointe du Toulinguet and Plage de Pen Hat

through park, then right along the cliff • Continue around the point, passing many traces of fortifications • 1.4kms do not join road but continue **R** on path down to meet road at **TJ**
EITHER go **R** to follow round headland **OR** for a short cut, descend road **ahead** to rejoin coast path at **P** **OR** having crossed road, bear **L** on path up to towers visible on brow of hill (Manoir de Coecilian)

MANOIR DE COECILIAN

This evocative skeleton was once the home of symbolist poet St-Pol-Roux. He named it after one of his sons who had died in WWI. In June 1940, German soldiers forced their way in, killed a servant and attacked the old man and his daughter. He died a few months later.

The Germans burnt all his books and papers and took over the house, which later attracted allied bombing and was finally left in ruins.

From the Manoir de Coecilian continue inland and across the road to see the Neolithic alignments

ALIGNMENTS DE LAGATJAR

The remains of a large scale Neolithic alignment, with more than 140 stones in straight lines, dominate the centre of the headland. The site dates from c3500BC and was probably used for ceremonial purposes in accordance with the movements of the sun, moon and changes of seasons.

Alignments of Lagatjar

Les Tas de Pois

27/3 From ⓟ at Plage de Pen Hat **CA** on path between fences (**60m on L - alternative route up to Manoir de Coecilian**) • Continue across grass behind beach, then follow up to cliff-top. • **CA** 1.5kms out to Pointe de Penhir (**passing Museum of the Battle of the Atlantic**) The line of rocks out to sea is called Les Tas de Pois (piles of peas)

MUSEUM OF THE BATTLE OF THE ATLANTIC   A concrete bunker houses this museum documenting the struggle between German U-boats and Allied navies during WWII, a sobering reminder of harsh realities around this exceptionally beautiful coast. Open April to October.

POINTE DE PEN-HIR   Breton resistance fighters are honoured here by a huge granite memorial, which was inaugurated by General de Gaulle in 1951.

• Go round point and descend to beach of Veryac'h • **CA** past crêperie down to ⓟ by slipway • Take path **ahead** up onto cliff • 100m at fork bear **R** • 200m bear **R** again, then follow stony path uphill • At top **CA**

27/4 At ⓟ behind cove, cross diagonally **L**, bear **R** through metal barrier onto path • 60m at junction

Kerloc'h

take middle path • Follow up onto cliff • **CA** on broad stony path
• 600m after Pointe de Portzen, fork **L** to **TJ** with track, follow this **R**
to continue on coast path • Ignore paths arriving from L, continue
down to houses at Kerloc'h • Just before tarmac road turn **R** down to
beach

27/5 Walk on sand or through P and along wide grassy verge beside
road • Through P at end, go up steps onto cliff • At junction of paths,
go **R** along edge of high, sheer cliffs – **attention!** • The vast sandy
beach of Kersiguénou is ahead • Path descends between hedges, then
bear **R** by wooden post to go along parallel with beach on dunes or on
sand • From P at end of beach **CA** on road • 250m at left bend, go **R**
uphill on narrow path through ferns • c350m path forks, go **R** to stay
near edge - **attention!** • Another fork, go **R** again • Another soon
after, keep along edge (**Confidence about heights is useful for this
path, but it is exceptional walking**)

27/6 Path drops down, runs level for a while, then climbs onto Pointe
de Dinan • Down and up steps above little cove • Bear **R** along wide
track • At junction of paths, go **R** (Possible to take shortcut to left to
cut out headland) • Follow any path round main headland and then on a
gradual descent to P at the foot

CHÂTEAU DE DINAN

This natural structure is called the Château de Dinan for obvious
reasons. It is possible to go right out onto the end over the arch, but
serious rock climbing and a good head for heights are required.
Legend associates this place with the mischievous Korrigans who
imprisoned their enemies the Giants in the caverns. Neolithic burial
chambers and artefacts were found in this area in the 19th century,
but much has since been lost through erosion and usage.

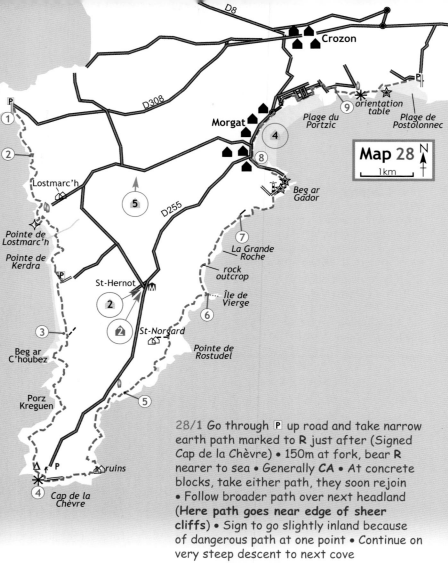

Map 28 N
1km

D8

Crozon

D308

P
①

②

Lostmarc'h

⑤

D255

Morgat

④

⑧

Plage du Portzic

⑨ orientation table

Plage de Postolonnec

P

Beg ar Gador

⑦

La Grande Roche

rock outcrop

Pointe de Lostmarc'h

Pointe de Kerdra

P

St-Hernot

②

②

St-Norgard

Île de Vierge

⑥

③

Beg ar C'houbez

Pointe de Rostudel

Porz Kreguen

⑤

P

ruins

④ Cap de la Chèvre

28/1 Go through P up road and take narrow earth path marked to **R** just after (Signed Cap de la Chèvre) • 150m at fork, bear **R** nearer to sea • Generally **CA** • At concrete blocks, take either path, they soon rejoin • Follow broader path over next headland (**Here path goes near edge of sheer cliffs**) • Sign to go slightly inland because of dangerous path at one point • Continue on very steep descent to next cove

28/2 Turn back up rocky track over ravine, then turn **R** soon after up steep path • Bear **R** soon after along wide track • At bend **CA** on narrow path going up over high cliff • Path continues along edge of cliff, then forks at top - **R** will follow edge, but go straight on if preferred • Approaching Lostmarc'h, make for signpost • Here turn **L** for 150m to see standing stones, then retrace steps and follow path to **R** onto headland

Lostmarc'h

Lostmarc'h, éperon barrée

LOSTMARC'H

This archaeological site comprises an éperon barré (c500BC), Neolithic alignments of menhirs, dolmens, and the remains of a settlement (oppidum). The outline of the fortifications on the spur is clearly visible from above as one approaches over the headland. A plaque at the end has a reconstruction drawing of what the camp might have looked like. The purpose of the large menhir on the cliff-top may have been to signal the presence of the alignments on the hillside behind.

This is also a significant geological location: on the south side of the north point of the peninsula here are distinctive formations known as pillow-lavas, the effect of lava oozing underwater out of the volcanic feeder in spurts like toothpaste from a tube. These round "pillows" are cemented by white limestone. They were formed by underwater eruption c.440 million years ago, at a time when a rift valley was opening in this area.

• **CA** above beach • Cross creek on metal bridge • **CA** across _Dunes Domaniales de Dinan_ on sandy path, with wooden fences protecting dunes • Bear **R** on path around headland, Pointe de Kerdra • **CA** above vast beach, Plage de la Palue • Go up wide stony track to **P**, bear **R** through it and keep going straight ahead (not down to the beach) • Where track turns **L** inland, go **R** through wooden posts, then **L** along coast path again • Immediately after, little squiggle **R** and then **L** to a narrow earth path along above dunes • Make for bridge crossing creek and **CA** behind dunes • This path goes up and down behind beach

Plage de Lostmarc'h

28/3 Turn inland briefly by sign for Beg Gou Armor, then **R** just after at junction of paths, towards Cap de la Chèvre • Keep on widest path going round nearest to edge of next point, Beg ar C'houbez • Path bears right on long slow climb over headland

The stone-walling is a legacy from reclaimed land at a time of population increase and agricultural expansion in the 19th century. As well as enclosing fields and penning animals, the walls were also a protection against erosion.

• Keep **ahead** • **(The semaphore station of Cap de la Chèvre can be seen in the distance)** Path turns inland around cove (Porz Kreguen), bears **R** along edge and descends • Up again opposite for very steep climb (or could stay on upper path) • Keep bearing **R** to continue along edge of cliffs • **Superb views of Cap Sizun and the Pointe du Van across the water** • After another big descent, path climbs onto last headland • **Towards the Cap there are laid paths, telescopes and viewing platforms**

CAP DE LA CHÈVRE

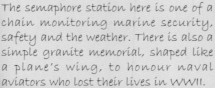

The semaphore station here is one of a chain monitoring marine security, safety and the weather. There is also a simple granite memorial, shaped like a plane's wing, to honour naval aviators who lost their lives in WWII.

28/4 Continue to **R** of semaphore station and go **ahead** on wide stony track • Round the Cap, a steep narrow path descends towards coves ahead, passing through an old ruined settlement with lavoir and overgrown houses • Path then climbs again: at fork go **ahead**, then prepare for sharp descent • Go inland round cove, ignoring paths coming down from road • Go straight on when the path divides near houses, and fork **R** after going under tree branch

28/5 Cross open heather-covered moorland (dolmen well inland near road) with views across to Île de l'Aber, then down to a large lavoir • Path then immediately turns **L** sharply and steeply uphill • Follow inland to cut out headland of Pointe de Rostudel (optional extra) • Keep straight up to top, ignoring little paths off to side, then through beautiful pine wood, high above water • At junction of paths, **CA** • **Île de Vierge ahead** • **CA** on main path • At fork with signboard, bear **R** • Later, path turns sharply **R** for steep drop towards water (**Care needed on slippery slope. Views of caves on l'Île de Vierge below**)

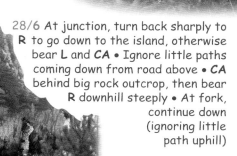

28/6 At junction, turn back sharply to **R** to go down to the island, otherwise bear **L** and **CA** • Ignore little paths coming down from road above • **CA** behind big rock outcrop, then bear **R** downhill steeply • At fork, continue down (ignoring little path uphill)

La Grande Roche

• Past more big rocks on edge of cliff • Path bends round **R** over stream, then **L** to climb again (**Very steep ascent up to another rocky pinnacle. This is a challenging stretch**) • Path turns inland behind La Grande Roche (**great bank of rock**) • **CA** on long open stretch, then back into pine wood for a section of easy walking

28/7 Attention: at fork, leave main path (ahead) and descend to **R** on slippery slope needing care • Path skirts property on cliff • Up very steep steps with rail • Path now level, open to sheer drop down to sea very long way below • Then path descends again • Come out at protected natural site of Beg ar Gador • Turn **L** inland (re-routed path, no access to grottoes below) • Pass **Calvaire du Gador (put up as a family's thanks for three sons surviving WWI)** • **CA** and at clearing turn **R** down avenue towards sea, past little lighthouse

BATTERY OF MORGAT This approach to the bay of Morgat was defended by three tiers of battery. The highest had a U-shaped platform (1757) and later guard-house, look-out post and powder store (now disappeared). The purpose was to prevent a landing which could lead to attacks on Brest via a land route.

• At the battery, follow the path to **R** – it eventually swings round and descends to the lower battery and fort • Then follow flat and easy path through trees, with great views of Morgat • Go down steps above harbour

THE FORT DU KADOR was a later addition to the defensive ensemble, and designed to be less visible from the sea. It is possible to go inside, but a protected colony of bats occupies part of the building.

• Bear **R** up from the fort on a broad path • At fork bear **R** downhill towards Morgat, descending to the harbour • Bear **R** at fork and down steps to the harbour

MORGAT

This charming town set around golden sands became popular with wealthy Parisians and foreigners in the 1920s. Many gracious houses remain on the surrounding hills in evidence of this period. It is now a perfect spot for active or lazy family holidays. The most famous attraction is a series of colourful marine grottoes, accessible by boat (Vedettes Rosmeur).

28/8 Bear **R** along the front • **CA** on main road, past traffic lights to roundabout • Bear **R** here and go through gates of Le Grand Hôtel de la Mer, past front of building, through Ⓟ and out of gates beyond • Continue to the **R** uphill at roundabout • 350m at top of rise, turn **R**, descending towards sea • Follow **L** along behind excellent swimming beach of Portzic • Turn **L** along Impasse St-Pol Roux, then **R** at next junction • Continue uphill and go **R** at **TJ** at top • 200m turn **L** (Rue St-Expury) • At the top of this road, turn **R** through a barrier towards the sea again

28/9 30m, go **L** at fork on narrow path signed Pointe du Menhir • At any junctions keep **ahead** along cliff, to Table of Orientation

Turn **L** inland here for just 40m to see the Menhir de la Républicaine which took its name from an old fort. The stone was destroyed by the Germans in WWII as it was used as a landmark for ships in the bay, but restored in 1992.

• Past orientation table, bear **R**, taking path downhill near rocky outcrop • 250m fork **R** sharply downhill towards edge of cliff • At bottom follow path ahead (now fenced), then turn **L** along coast • Follow path **L** by former Fort de Postolonnec (1860), now private house • Go under amazing tree growing over path • Bear **L** at fork, then **R** immediately to continue along coast • At road, turn **R** • **CA** by beach to Ⓟ at end

8. PRACTICAL INFORMATION

SHOPS & SERVICES
- **Landévennec** - (épicerie, limited hours/depot pain, refreshments)
- **Lanveoc** www.lanveoc.presquile-crozon.com
- **Camaret** TO 02.98.27.93.60 www.camaretsurmer-tourisme.fr
- **Crozon & Morgat** TO 02 98 27 07 92 www.presquile-crozon.com Mkt Wed

ACCOMMODATION
Chambres d'hôte
1. Trouz Ar Mor (400m) 29570 Camaret 02 98 27 83 57
www.trouzarmor.com

Chambres d'hôte & Gîte d'étape
2. Jacqueline Le Guillou (1.1km) Gîtes de St-Hernot, 29160 Crozon
02 98 27 15 00

Rando-Gîte
3. Rando-Gîte de Landévennec (100m) 02 98 27 72 65

Rando-Plume
4. Rando-Plume Ouest Découverte (50m) 29160 Morgat 02 98 26 22 11
www.ouest-decouvertes.com

5. Rando-Plume Kastell Dinn (2kms) Hameau de Kerluantec, 29160 Morgat
02 98 27 26 40 Open all year

Camping
6. Camping de Trez Rouz (100m) Route de Camaret à Roscanvel, 29160
Crozon 02 98 27 93 96 www.trezrouz.com March-October
7. Camping de la Plage de Goulien (100m) Kernavéno, 29160 Crozon
02 98 26 23 16

TRANSPORT
Bus services: Infrequent bus services connect Camaret, Crozon and
Morgat – see www.viaoo29.fr
Taxi: Kermarec 02 98 27 11 85 Crozon

Boat trips to grottoes at Morgat – Vedettes Rosmeur
www.grottes-morgat.com

Boats to islands of Sein, Molène and Ouessant in summer season –
Penn ar Bed, quai Téphany, 29570 Camaret 02 98 27 88 22
www.pennarbed.com

OTHER WALKS
10km circuit from Landévennec to Le Loc'h following coast, then
returning across country via hamlet of La Forêt.

A 12km walking circuit can be followed from point 27/**5** to Lostmarc'h
along the coast and then back across country.

10km circuit of the Pointe des Espagnols from Roscanvel fort.

9. L'Aber-Douarnenez
The Bay of Douarnenez
41 kms

The huge curve of the Bay of Douarnenez offers mostly easy walking, apart from one very steep short climb at the Falaises de Guern. Long sandy swimming beaches, such as my favourite at Pen Trez, backed by numerous camping sites abound. The sea and the scenery are the stars here rather than much man-made interest, with views of both the Crozon peninsula to the north and Cap Sizun to the south. Geology enthusiasts will enjoy the rock faces around the old lime kiln and L'Aber peninsula.

The town of Douarnenez, goal of this section, is a lively fishing port with a particular niche in French political history. It also yields a remarkable Gallo-Roman site and a living boat museum where visitors can scramble about above and below decks of various vessels. This is one place I am always happy to have an excuse to visit.

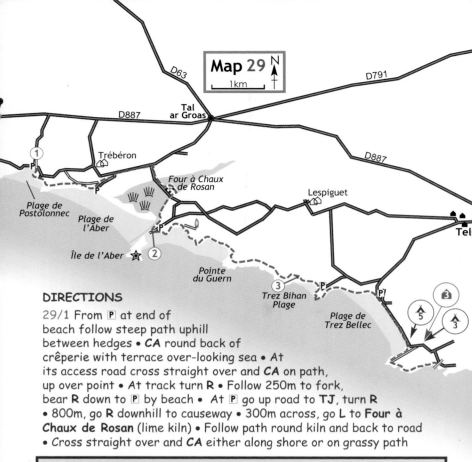

DIRECTIONS

29/1 From **P** at end of
beach follow steep path uphill
between hedges • **CA** round back of
crêperie with terrace over-looking sea • At
its access road cross straight over and **CA** on path,
up over point • At track turn **R** • Follow 250m to fork,
bear **R** down to **P** by beach • At **P** go up road to **TJ**, turn **R**
• 800m, go **R** downhill to causeway • 300m across, go **L** to **Four à
Chaux de Rosan** (lime kiln) • Follow path round kiln and back to road
• Cross straight over and **CA** either along shore or on grassy path

---

FOUR À CHAUX DE ROSAN

This lime-kiln was established in 1839 and worked for the next forty
years, producing lime for agricultural or construction purposes from
the limestone quarry beside it. Here an open rock face preserves the
pillow lavas which indicate underwater volcanic activity (see p.121)
c.440 million years ago.

Looking back from Pointe du Guern

ÎLE DE L'ABER

This island is cut off at high tide, so beware of lingering too long to explore the former Iron Age defences and a fort of 1862 with barracks and an artillery platform above. The building's distinctive appearance is due to the use of dolorite, an unusual choice for construction.

above • After c.700m there is causeway out to the Île de l'Aber, accessible at low tide

29/2 Continue **L** over the rocks onto a track and then **R** before road and P • Follow path ahead 650m, then just before track turn sharp **R** downhill **(or CA on track 150m to see two menhirs L of track and another further on to R – return same way)** • Stay on this path bearing R/straight ahead at junctions for 1.5km • Past a noticeboard, turn **L** through trees for very steep climb to Pointe du Guern • At top go **R** to go out to point (if desired), otherwise keep **ahead**, through pine woods, very high above the water

29/3 At fork in path after 1.4km, at clearing in pine wood, bear **R** downhill for very steep descent – **care needed on zig-zag path** • This comes out above beach of Trez Bihan • Bear **R** before P to **CA** on path above beach • Follow out onto little headland, wiggling round the contours (or cut straight across if preferred) • Turn inland towards vast beach of Trez Bellec • Keep ahead at any junctions of paths • At road turn **R**, then through a grassy area to **CA** on road above beach **(or just go along the sand for well over a kilometre)** • At end of beach where road turns inland, turn **R** along coastal path • At track, go **R** • At end, follow path **L**, round edge of fields 1km • At road go **R**

30/1 After 250m turn **R**, immediately before house at Roz ar Greis • Follow **L** along coast

Falaises du Guern

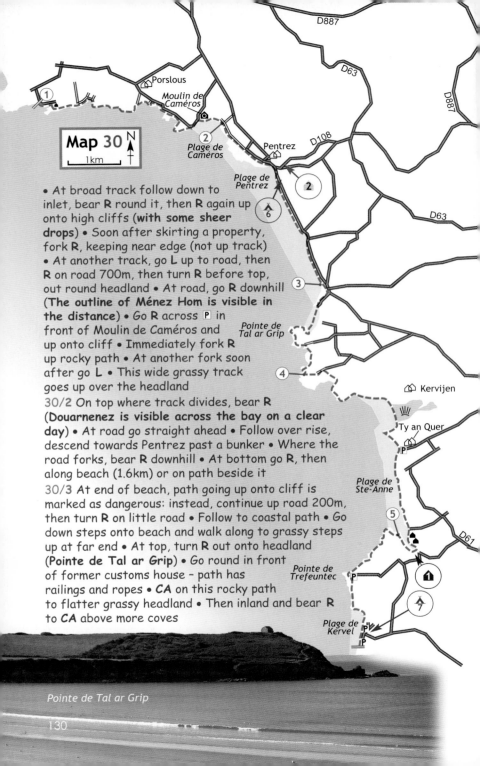

Map 30 N

1km

- At broad track follow down to inlet, bear **R** round it, then **R** again up onto high cliffs (**with some sheer drops**) • Soon after skirting a property, fork **R**, keeping near edge (not up track) • At another track, go **L** up to road, then **R** on road 700m, then turn **R** before top, out round headland • At road, go **R** downhill (**The outline of Ménez Hom is visible in the distance**) • Go **R** across P in front of Moulin de Caméros and up onto cliff • Immediately fork **R** up rocky path • At another fork soon after go **L** • This wide grassy track goes up over the headland

30/2 On top where track divides, bear **R** (**Douarnenez is visible across the bay on a clear day**) • At road go straight ahead • Follow over rise, descend towards Pentrez past a bunker • Where the road forks, bear **R** downhill • At bottom go **R**, then along beach (1.6km) or on path beside it

30/3 At end of beach, path going up onto cliff is marked as dangerous: instead, continue up road 200m, then turn **R** on little road • Follow to coastal path • Go down steps onto beach and walk along to grassy steps up at far end • At top, turn **R** out onto headland (**Pointe de Tal ar Grip**) • Go round in front of former customs house – path has railings and ropes • **CA** on this rocky path to flatter grassy headland • Then inland and bear **R** to **CA** above more coves

Porslous
Moulin de Caméros
Plage de Caméros
Pentrez
Plage de Pentrez
Pointe de Tal ar Grip
Kervijen
Ty an Quer
Plage de Ste-Anne
Pointe de Trefeuntec
Plage de Kervel

D887
D63
D887
D108
D63
D61

Pointe de Tal ar Grip

Marshes at Kervijen

30/4 Path turns inland and joins track • Go ahead, then at road bear **R** on path • *CA* bearing **R** at forks (and ignoring little access road to beach) • Follow round headland, then along side of cliff • Descend to beach and follow path behind it (**marsh on the left**)

The marshland at Kervijen has been planted with reeds designed to absorb polluted water before it reaches the sea.

• Cross stream on bridge, then bear **R** up around headland • Descend to ℙ at Ty an Quer • *CA* above beach or on sand, keeping **L** of building • Keep ahead along edge of fencing to inlet, then bear **R** along sand in front of buildings • Continue 100m past last house, then go up rocks to take narrow path above inlet • At end, just bear **R** round top and follow out onto headland

LOST CITY OF YS

Brittany's Atlantis legend is associated with the bay of Douarnenez. The city of Ys was built by King Gradlon for his daughter Dahut, when she tired of the rather staid living in Quimper, where St-Corentin was her father's main advisor. But Ys became a place of such dissolute pleasure that punishment and disaster were inevitable. A mysterious lover presented himself to Dahut and persuaded her to give him the key to the sluice-gates that protected the city from the surrounding waves. Once these were opened, Ys was in peril of vanishing beneath the sea. When Dahut tried to escape, her father took pity and carried her from the rising water on his horse, but St-Corentin intervened and Gradlon was forced to abandon her and the city to the waves. Fishermen in later times claim to have heard the ghostly ringing of bells from the lost city.

Kervel

30/5 In trees where path forks, go **L** uphill • At next fork, go **R** to go round headland (or **L** to cut it out) • *CA* along series of low cliffs • At an enclosure go **R**, then **L** round it (although shortcut has been forced through fence) • **Views across to the Cap de la Chèvre and the Pointe du Van** • At Pointe de Trefeuntec, go **L** into P, across its corner, and *CA* on path • Descend to Plage de Kervel, following path in front of houses to P • Cross P to road, bear **R** 60m to next P
• **Refreshments here in season**

31/1 From P, go ahead along path above beach • 150m before promontory, turn **L** onto little road, then go **R**, along edge of P and **ahead** on grassy path • **EITHER** pass behind cross over hill-top (Beg ar Gorred) **OR** go up to cross and turn **L** just before it

---

ABBÉ JULIEN BERNARD (d.1944)

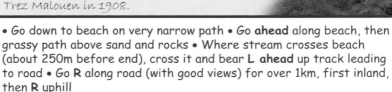

The cross honours a man who devoted his life to improving that of others. In 1905 he created a sporting branch for the association Championnet which helped to promote popular education. Thanks to his efforts, the first holiday centre for disadvantaged children was built here at Ker Trez Malouen in 1908.

• Go down to beach on very narrow path • Go **ahead** along beach, then grassy path above sand and rocks • Where stream crosses beach (about 250m before end), cross it and bear **L ahead** up track leading to road • Go **R** along road (with good views) for over 1km, first inland, then **R** uphill

31/2 At top, go **R** at junction • Go **R** at next junction • 200m turn **R** at main road • Carry on up main road (**OR make a very short detour to beach with information board, then return to the road**)

The noticeboard recalls the association of surrealist painter Yves Tanguy (1900-1955) with this area. Born in Paris of Breton parents he retained a strong connection with his roots. One of his most famous paintings, Multiplication des Arcs, was inspired by walks around Douarnenez. He died in America, but his widow stipulated in her will a few years later, that her ashes and those of her husband should be scattered in the bay here.

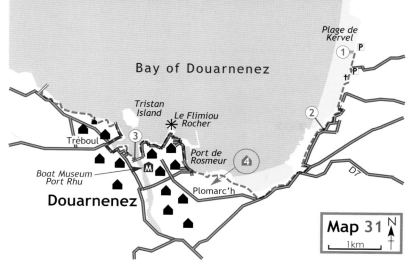

Bay of Douarnenez

Plage de Kervel

Tristan Island

Le Flimiou Rocher

Tréboul

Boat Museum
Port Rhu

Douarnenez

Port de Rosmeur

Plomarc'h

D7

Map 31 N

1km

• Continue up steep road • At top by junction go **R** down steps onto footpath • Keep ahead through wood high above water, entering the atmospheric area of the Plomarc'h • 650m, see remains of Roman garum factory on **R** • Keep **ahead** between some old houses, follow footpath beside wall (ignoring access road to L) • Just before stone lavoir, go sharp **R** by large tree, step across stream and bear **L** ahead **• The old village and the farm are soon just to the L here – either make a detour or CA on narrow path** • At end, go up steps, then **R** along road • At next junction, bear **R** downhill • At end, go **R** again,

PLOMARC'H This green oasis of peace has many viewpoints over the changing light of the Bay of Douarnenez and much of interest to see. It has long been a place of inspiration for artists and poets, such as Boudin, Sérusier and Max Jacob. At the eastern end are the remains of a Gallo-Roman industrial complex, dating from the 2-3rd centuries AD, where garum (a Roman delicacy - fish sauce made from rotting entrails) was produced for export. Steps at the corner go down to a tiny creek once used to trap fish by means of an enclosing wall and removeable grill (ar Gored is the Breton term for this type of fishery), so that low tide left them stranded.

Further on, two hamlets also remain, with ancient houses and a large stone lavoir. These once housed workers in the sardine industry, basket-weavers, rope-makers and other craftsmen. There is also a gîte d'étape today and a working farm with many animals on show.

Port de Rosmeur

DOUARNENEZ

This is a town of three ports: Rosmeur, the working fishing harbour, Tréboul, packed with pleasure boats, and in between, the living boat museum of Port de Rhu. The latter has an exceptional display of working boats and boating paraphernalia inside, and further examples on the water which visitors can explore.

The development of Douarnenez over the centuries has marched alongside its role as centre of the sardine industry. An exceptional richness of plankton in the bay attracts millions of fish each year between May and November and the prosperity of the town has been closely allied with this. The disappearance of sardine stocks between 1902 and 1912 caused enormous hardship, forcing the local fishermen to adapt to new methods and new waters to fill the gap. Industrialised conservation of sardines began in earnest in 1860, with the necessary salt, wood for barrels and oil being imported. Canning factories grew up later, providing much employment.

This fishing tradition became a focus for the radical political action strongly featured in the town's history. In 1921 Sébastien Velly became the first communist mayor in the whole of France, and he was succeeded by a comrade, Daniel le Flanchec, on his death soon after. 1924 saw a strike by sardine workers at the Usine Carnaud over appalling pay and conditions: a tense struggle with the bosses turned to violence and destruction after an attempt was made on the life of the mayor. One of the strike leaders, Joséphine Pencalet was voted into local office the following year, despite the illegality of women's participation in politics at that time.

There is still an atmosphere of energy and engagement in the town, which has much to ffer visitors and is also the home of that excellent, and highly recommended magazine of all things Breton, Armen.

TRISTAN ISLAND

The name Douarnenez means 'land of the island' suggesting early offshore settlement here. The legendary association is with the hero Tristan, nephew of King Marc'h (or Mark), who fell in love with his uncle's bride after drinking a magic potion. Wagner's opera 'Tristan und Isolde' recounts their tragic story, which is an earlier tale than the Arthurian romances it is often associated with.

Historically, the most infamous holder of the island, Guy Eder de la Fontenelle, arrived in 1595. This young man became the scourge of the whole area, taking advantage of the turbulent times as the Wars of Religion raged throughout France, to raid and burn entire villages, killing and plundering at whim, apparently for pleasure as much as profit. He managed to secure the pardon of Henri IV in 1598 and was allowed to keep control of his island. Before long, however, he was involved in political intrigues with the Spaniards and was finally executed in Paris in 1602 at the age of 29.

then bear **L** along front by port, past bars and restaurants. **The fishing and canning industry still function here at the Port de Rosmeur. It is also the base of the Vedettes de Rosmeur for boat-trips around the bay.**

• Keep ahead (ignore ramp uphill) into port area • Follow road round to **L**, then go straight over at junction between commercial buildings • At end, **EITHER** go **R** to climb Flimiou Rocher for views, **OR** continue **L**,

Port Rhu, boat museum

then **R** to bear round a couple of little bays • **Tristan island is just ahead (see p.135)** • The road eventually turns up the estuary with views of Tréboul, the pleasure port • Continue to passerelle, turn **R** across this (**NB or visit The Port Musée first, just ahead here**)

31/3 At far end turn **R** • At road, bear **R** for a short way, then go **R** down footpath and bear **L** alongside the water • Follow road round top of harbour of Tréboul • At end of harbour, take No-Through-Road to **R**, continuing by water • Road becomes track: just before end, go **L** up footpath with railings • **CA** on same path along coast above sandy cove, then up to Chapelle de St-Jean

---

MEMORIAL OF MAX JACOB

This Quimper-born poet and painter, friend of Picasso, was a notable figure in Parisian artistic circles in the first half of the 20th century, whilst retaining strong links with his Breton roots. Jacob often stayed in the hotel Ty Mad by the chapel here and brought many of his friends, including the young English modernist painter Kit Wood, who painted some of his best seascapes in this part of Brittany. Wood was an opium addict, and fell under a train in Salisbury under the influence of the drug in 1930. His short life was one of the three subjects of Sebastian Faulks' interesting book The Fatal Englishman.

This two-headed memorial to Max Jacob represents contrasting aspects: that of the worldly artist on the one hand, and the reflective convert from Judaism to Catholicism on the other. He died in a Nazi concentration camp in 1944.

• Go to **R** of chapel and **CA**, soon going along beach behind wall • At end, cross beach (Les Sables Blancs) and **CA** along promenade behind sea wall • 300m turn **L** up steps to **P**, then turn **R** up road • 300m turn **R** by parking sign • Continue through **P** and to **L** of tennis court to rejoin coastal path

9. PRACTICAL INFORMATION

SHOPS & SERVICES
- **St-Nic** TO 02 98 26 55 15
- **Telgruc-sur-Mer** TO 02 98 27 78 06
- **Douarnenez** TO 02 98 92 13 35 www.douarnenez-tourisme.com
  Mkt Mon (fresh produce in the halles every morning)

ACCOMMODATION

Hotels

1. Rand' Hôtel de Relais de Tréfeuntec (on route) 02 98 92 50 03.
   29550 Plonévez Porzay

Chambres d'hôte

2. Mme Renée Gouriten (50m) 02 98 26 50 38. 8 rue de la plage,
   Pentrez, 29550 Saint Nic www.chambres-pentrez.com

Gîte d'étape

3. Centre Nautique (on route) Plage de Trez Bellec, 29560 Telgruc-sur-
   Mer 02 98 27 33 83 (camping here too)

4. Ferme des Plomarc'h (on route) 29100 Douarnenez 02 98 92 75 41
   www.mairie-douarnenez.fr Open all year

Camping

5. Camping Pen Bellec (on route) Plage de Trez Bellec, 29560 Telgruc-
   sur-Mer 02 98 27 31 87 Open June – September

6. Camping Ker Ys (on route) Pentrez Plage, 29550 Saint-Nic
   02 98 26 53 95 www.ker-ys.com

8. Camping La Ville d'Ys (100m) Plage de Kervel 02 98 92 50 52
   Open May - September

TRANSPORT

Bus services: Douarnenez TO to Quimper - www.voyages-sncf.com
   Other services see www.viaoo29.fr

Taxi: Alain Jolec 02 98 81 26 77 Plomodiern
   François Ferrant 02 98 74 37 37 Douarnenez

Boat trips: Vedettes de Rosmeur (trips around Bay of Douarnenez,
   Goulien bird reserve, fishing) Port de Pêche, 29173 Douarnenez
   02 98 92 83 83 www.pennsardin.com

OTHER WALKS

12km coast and country circuit Tal-ar-
Groas (via L'Aber)

GR37 via Pentrez leads to link with
Ménez Hom circuit of 13kms

4km circuit of Douarnenez, including the
Plomarc'h

For full details of these walks, see
Walking and other Activities in Finistere

10. Douarnenez - Ménez-Drégan
Cap Sizun
73 kms

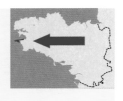

It is hard to imagine now the political struggles around Plogoff in 1980 to prevent the location of a nuclear power station on this stark peninsula. The protest rallies and passionate opposition remain captured in popular songs and a film, Des Pierres contre des Fusils (Stones against Guns).

For coastal walking Cap Sizun is a remarkably scenic and challenging prospect! There are plenty of demanding stretches with swift changes of gradient to negotiate stream valleys punctuating the very high cliffs. Some scrambling over boulders and slippery rocks may be necessary in places, particularly on the first section from Douarnenez to the Pointe de Penharn. A series of spurs fortified in the Iron Age and vast gorse or heather-covered moors reflect the rugged nature of the northern coast. Care should be taken at all times on the cliffs, and especially in high winds.

In good weather there are excellent views to the Cap de la Chèvre and, from the Pointe du Raz, out to the Île de Sein, an almost flat island still managing to keep its head above the stormy Atlantic waters. The nature reserve of Goulien will be a major attraction for avid bird-watchers. A blessed lack of development on the actual coastline results in splendidly isolated walking, but also the concomitant drawback of having to go some distance inland for supplies and accommodation. Planning in advance is therefore recommended for long-distance trekking here.

Pointe du Raz

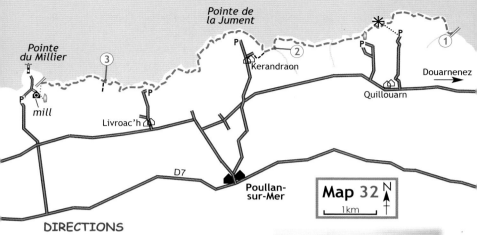

DIRECTIONS

32/1 **CA** on coastal path, round head of cove, then **R** across stream • **CA**, bearing **R** (ignore paths to L) • Where path suddenly turns uphill and forks – go **R** • **CA** 500m, look **L** 50m for large menhir • **CA** 1.5km

32/2 At pretty tree-lined rectangular bay, follow path inland round head of stream • Go down and up over another stream valley (**another difficult stretch with rock clambering required**) • At fork, go **R** and continue round Pointe de la Jument • **CA** 3kms

32/3 At fork in path, go **R** (can see Pointe du Millier ahead) • 1.3km descend to valley (below mill) and cross to track • **DIVERSION**: follow sign **L** to old mill (Moulin de Keriolet, see next page)

Pointe du Millier

MOULIN DE KERIOLET

It is well worth a short (and shady) break to see the idyllic sylvan setting of the Moulin de Keriolet (1868), an old mill with an 8m metal wheel now restored to working order. It is open during the afternoons in July and August. The delightful stream has its own mini granite 'chaos' – step across the boulders and up a bank to see the 'stone boat' in which St-Conogan (allegedly) reached these shores.
The two great rocks here may be fallen menhirs.

33/1 From valley go **R** (or ahead if returning from mill) up around Pointe du Millier • **CA** up steps to pass behind lighthouse compound • At road, turn **R** by garage onto path • **CA** along cliffs, ignoring paths to **L** • **Over next headland the town of Beuzec comes into view, just over 3kms away as the crow flies** • **CA** for 2kms to Plage du Pors Peron • Follow down to beach and across sand to end of road • Go up road 75m • **(CA for camping)** Turn **R** towards telephone box, then **R** beyond it • Follow track between houses and **CA** • Behind next cove do not join road - turn **R** instead on path • Follow over next headland to another rocky cove • Cross road and **P** to **CA** on coast path for 1km to Pte de Trenaouret • Past this, climb over gap in stone wall

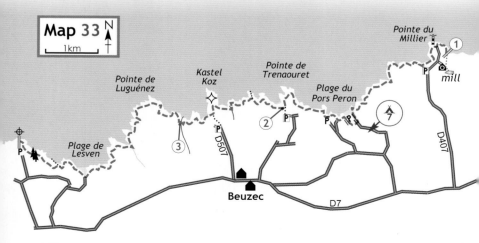

Kastel Koz

33/2 CA around top of very deep cove: on other side, follow smaller path **R** • After next cove, at fork go **L** (**R goes out to point only**) • **Kastel Koz now in view** • At headland before this, path crosses flat rock, apparently over cliff-edge - continue with care and path soon becomes clear again • **CA** into head of valley, across stream

KASTEL KOZ Although no traces remain today, Kastel Koz was once the site of a Gallic 'oppidum', according to artefacts found during excavations of this éperon barré. The natural defences of the site were augmented with ditches and banks in the Iron Age, to protect a settlement of about 200 habitations.

• Behind Kastel Koz follow path sharp **L** inland, back up natural causeway • 200m **CA** uphill, ignoring path on **R** • Bear **R** towards fence, then turn **R** at it to **CA** on coast path

33/3 Follow path into ravine, then back down to bridge • **CA** up steps on other side • Follow around Pte de Luguénez (**ruined Maison de garde just behind the coast path**) • **CA** 1km to cross another ravine by bridge • **CA** to Plage de Lesven • Cross road behind beach • **CA** over next headland • At fork in grassy path behind cove, bear **L** on higher path • Cross stream, **CA** around next headland • Descend again towards conifer plantation • Follow through top of plantation, and **CA** to next headland • At face of headland follow sharp **L** and over rocky point • **CA** past sea-mark pillar far below (**Path on L climbs to** P)

34/1 Keep ahead, ignoring little paths to **L** • 300m path comes to very steep descent and ascent • A little way up slope, path forks and rejoins soon after • Go across top of headland, on edge of field and follow grassy track ahead • At access road and P for **Réserve de Goulien Cap-Sizun** go ahead on path by fencing, parallel with road • Where fencing ends, keep **ahead** on this path, moving nearer cliff edge to go round cove • At fork go **ahead** inland, ignoring path to **L** • Then follow back out towards sea

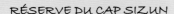

RÉSERVE DU CAP SIZUN

This bird reserve was started in the 1950s by Michel-Hervé Julien. Now a protected area covering 40 hectares, it includes moorland, cliffs and offshore rocky islets. Parts are closed during autumn and winter and during the breeding season, but the coastal path does pass through reserve territory. Gulls, choughs, crested cormorants, fulmars, razorbills and many others make their homes here.

34/2 Path soon turns **L** and then – **attention** - turn **R** downhill almost immediately after (**easy to miss**)
• **CA** over stream and up again,
• At track, go **R** towards house on cliff edge • Turn **L** before it, downhill very steeply and inevitably up again • Go through gate into reserve territory and **CA**, soon across an open headland and through another gate • **CA** bearing **R** • Descend again (two ways, one directly, one snaking) to cross head of inlet • Very narrow path going inland, then across headland • This becomes track – keep ahead

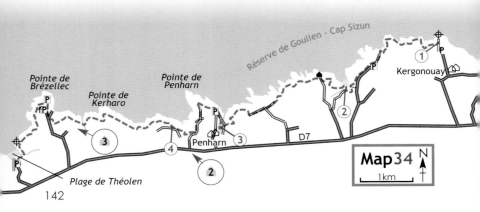

• Join another track, bear **R** and ahead • Stay on it, eventually turning **R** 90°, back out to headland • Follow very narrow and overgrown path • Descend to track • Turn **L** inland to go up to head of valley (Penharn)

34/3 Cross stream, then turn back sharply up rough steps • At 3-way fork of paths, take middle one **ahead** • Come up onto track and **CA** uphill • Bear **R** downhill soon after • Go **R** at a track • At top, cross P and go ahead on path out onto Pointe de Penharn • From grassy open space before end, follow path back sharply to **L** (can go **R** out to end) • Follow wide stony track 400m and go **R** at fork • Turn **R** off track onto narrow path • 400m turn **R** along track

34/4 100m turn **R**, back onto path • **CA** on easy path round Pointe de Kerharo, then ahead skirting coves towards Pointe de Brezellec (one descend and ascent quite steep) • Path then runs alongside wall to Brezellec - **CA** on path nearest edge • Make way round deep cove (Baie de Brezellec) with tiny harbour below • At road, ignore first road to **R** downhill and take second one alongside wire fencing to P • Continue on footpath from right-hand corner of P

TORAN IROISE This compound once housed a centre of the Toran Iroise radionavigation system (now out-dated), for precise locations in the Mer Iroise and Bay of Biscay.

• **CA** round headland on broad stony track • At end bear **L** through another P up over rocks • Keep ahead, going inland round coves and then back again

143

Looking west from Pointe de Brézellec

(seamark on rocks before Théolen soon comes into view) • Follow path behind seamark, inland around cove, then snaking down steep slope, over stream and sharply up • Bear **R** to continue round next little headland • **(On turning inland the other daymark for alignment is visible on hill above)** • Come out from behind houses onto **P** at Théolen • Buvette here for refreshments

seamark

buvette

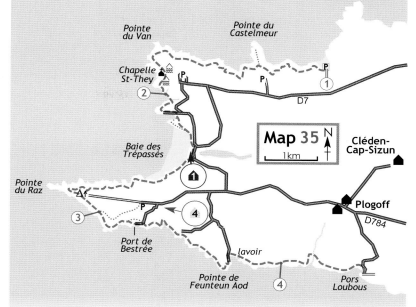

Map 35

N
1km

35/1 Cross 🅿 and **CA** on footpath up onto next headland • **CA** on this same path nearest the edge • Where path forks just past a stone wall, go **R** down to cliff edge again (**looking across to Castelmeur éperon barré**) • Keep to **R** of stone wall (**Pointe de Van visible ahead**) • Continue to Castelmeur – out to end if desired to see ditches and site of oppidum (see below) - otherwise, **CA** • Follow path **ahead** across rocks and heather to Pointe du Van, bearing **R** to keep close to edge • At fork of paths by stone wall, take **R** fork

CASTELMEUR

Another éperon barré, certainly in use during the Iron Age as weapons found here show, but possibly a much older fortified site. Defences consisted of four banks and three ditches, with habitations placed on the east and west slopes behind. 95 of these were found in late 19th century excavations - look for rectangles where the vegetation grows much greener. Evidence suggested that they were eventually destroyed by fire.

Looking back from Castelmeur

145

POINTE DU VAN The paths around the point itself are fairly smooth and gravelled – visitors to this popular spot are asked to keep to the marked routes to prevent erosion. There are various choices of route around the headland. From here there are views across to the opposite Pointe du Raz and out to the Île de Sein.

CHAPELLE DE ST-THEY

Little is known of St-They, a 6th century follower of St-Guénolé. The T of his name has mutated from D (Dei) – in Cornwall his name is St-Day. According to local legend, the chapel bell sounds spontaneously to warn sailors of danger.

• Follow signs to pass **Chapelle de St-They** on cliff-edge (its fontaine a few paces off to left of path) • Then bear **R** along the cliffs, past another fontaine • Path now follows a steep and rocky route - pay particular attention round cove of grass-covered rock stacks

35/2 Cross stream and bear **L** up next cliff • Further round cove, descend steeply, follow wide grassy path a little way, then bear **R** downhill on narrow path • Cross another stream and bear **L** up rocks • **CA**, then bear **L** to road below • Follow road **L** 400m, then turn **R** onto path again • 150m at fork, go **L** to cut out the headland, or **R** for challenging route round edge • Path descends steeply to Baie des Trépassés • At road bear **R**, then **R** at main road • **CA** past hotel on beach, then bear **R** up sandy dune path between fences, continuing steeply uphill to **R** of bunker

BAIE DES TREPASSÉS (Bay of the Dead)

The name of this beautiful bay probably results from a linguistic corruption, confusing the Breton Anaon (the dead) with An Aon (the river). Certainly it has developed legends to fit the former interpretation, with stories ranging from Druidic burials on the Île de Sein to the sound of the mournful cries of Dahut's dead lovers (see p.131) and the more prosaic location for the retrieval of the bodies of drowned seafarers. The river which now flows out from Le Loch, may once have entered the sea at this point. The Baie des Trepassés lies on a geological fault line which runs across Brittany from the Landes de Lanvaux and through Quimper right to the end of this peninsula.

• **CA** on path undulating across steep hillside (**the top of signals station at Point du Raz is soon visible ahead**) • After steep climb up very rocky section, walking is fairly easy all the way to the point, which is reached across a plateau of heather-covered moorland • Towards 19th century semaphore station, at fork in path, bear **R** to

POINTE DU RAZ

This protected area has its visitor centre (information / refreshments / shops / facilities) set 1km back from the point to preserve the natural splendour of one of the most visited sites in France. (Shame about the statue.) It is not, however, the most westerly point – see p.74

Across the often turbulent waters of the Raz de Sein, the island of Sein can be seen in good visibility.

go to point • It is possible to climb out along the precarious rocky ridges to the very end, but signs do warn of the risk • **CA** round headland on roughly paved path to statue of Notre-Dames des Naufragés (the Shipwrecked Ones) • Bear **R** here to continue on the coastal path

35/3 500m at fork in path go **R** to continue on coastal path (**L back to** P **and visitor centre**) • Keep bearing **R**, nearest to cliff edge (**very narrow path with fairly sheer drop**) • At fork above the little harbour of Bestrée,

EITHER go **R** steeply downhill to steps to road, then **L** up road 200m
OR just go straight ahead and reach road where coastal path goes off
to **R** (**A spectacularly placed seat is just ahead**) • Where path forks at wooden sign, bear **R** • After passing next little bay, there is a steep climb, then a stretch right on cliff edge • **CA** (path peppered with little rocks to trip the unwary) • Approaching Pointe du Feunteun Aod, bear **R** where path divides • **CA** to steep slipway, and join road • 300m turn **R** onto path by picnic table • Past this, bear **R** • At lavoir, cross top wall to other side (**concrete rain shelter here**) • Approaching next headland, bear **R** where path divides

35/4 At next cove, descend to railing, then up steps on other side
• At another cove, go through wooden barrier, follow path inland uphill
• As water-tower comes into sight ahead, turn off sharp **R** and descend to cross stream behind cove • **CA** on main path to next cove
• Follow zig-zags (to avoid a bad section) then climb to cliffs overlooking Pors Loubous • Here join road and follow **R** down towards harbour (**Note the stele to L set in the wall here**)

This stele is in memory of three French officers who landed here secretly from London, and were later shot by the Germans in August 1941 after betrayal by a double-agent. Honoré Estienne d'Orves was a famous resistance hero – a street in Brest on this walking route is also named after him.

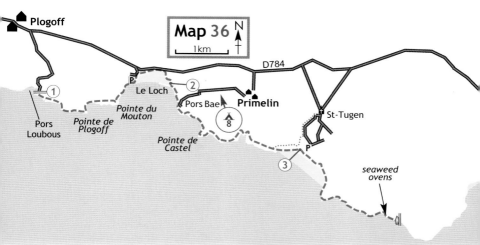

36/1 Turn **L** along coastal path • **CA** along often rocky path • Bear **R** at forks to go round series of headlands • At Pointe de Plogoff follow path inland through ferns at head of rocky bay • Then turn **R** uphill again, keeping **R** at forks • Pointe du Mouton ahead has little lookout house (with seat) on cliff edge • Continue down to cross shingly beach 30m then bear **L** on path again along edge of low cliffs • Continue up

PARC NATUREL MARIN D'IROISE

Go-ahead was given in late 2007 for the first marine park in France, covering 3550km² and stretching from Ouessant to the Île de Sein, including the coastline between (but excluding the Rade de Brest). Its aims are to achieve the delicate balance of protecting the environment whilst allowing sustainable activities to develop. Emphasis will be given to studying the natural riches of the area, maintaining the physical legacies of maritime history and supporting human activities from fishing and seaweed collection to tourism.

The scheme is not without its opponents, who anticipate outside interference and over-regulation of local practices, but it is generally welcomed by environmentalists.

Harbour at Le Loc'h

past [P] and keep ahead • At track, go **L** to road • Follow **R** 50m • Bear **R** onto footpath, follow round to beach at Le Loc'h • Go **ahead** on main road, then fork off **R** onto footpath to end of beach

36/2 **CA** behind harbour • Follow round headland • At Pors Bae, go **R** along road 100m, then **R** on path again • Continue round Pointe de Castel and large double cove further on • Ignore path off to left (which goes up to Chapelle de St-Tugen, about 1.2kms away) • Descend to large sandy beach

CHAPELLE DE ST-TUGEN This exceptional chapel in its walled enclosure (enclos paroissal), dating from 1535, is well worth a visit when it is open in the summer months.

36/3 Cross a little bridge, bear **L** 50m, following wire fence up and round over grassy dunes • Follow path behind house, then **CA** alongside wire fence in V round gully • At end of beach, bear **R** round headland (passing a rogue canon embedded in the ground)

• Follow easy path along low cliffs • **CA**, with walled enclosures to **L**, a series of rocky bays unfolding ahead • **At open grassy space there is a menhir on the cliff-edge and several seaweed ovens. The wooden posts resting on upright stone slabs are for hauling wicker baskets of seaweed from the beach below.**

150

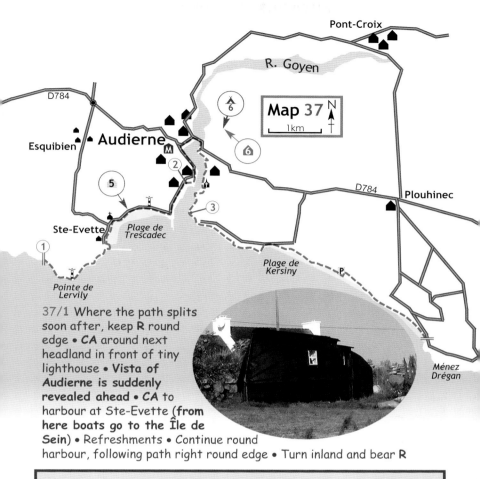

Map 37 N

1km

Pont-Croix

R. Goyen

D784

Esquibien
Audierne
M
②
⑤
③
⑥
⑥

Plouhinec

D784

Ste-Evette
Plage de Trescadec

①

Pointe de Lervily

Plage de Kersiny
P

Ménez Drégan

37/1 Where the path splits soon after, keep **R** round edge • **CA** around next headland in front of tiny lighthouse • **Vista of Audierne is suddenly revealed ahead** • **CA** to harbour at Ste-Evette (**from here boats go to the Île de Sein**) • Refreshments • Continue round harbour, following path right round edge • Turn inland and bear **R**

CHAPELLE DE ST-EVETTE

Ste-Evette and St-Démet were saved from shipwreck near here on their journey from England. They built a hermitage in thanks for their safety but were told they must separate. According to the legend, the saint travelled on to this spot in a stone boat.

Port at Ste-Evette

MOLENEZ

151

AUDIERNE

A stroll around this attractive port on the Goyen estuary reveals the essence of its maritime history, from the 17th century houses of armateurs (wealthy ship-owners/merchants) to the ship motif in relief sculpture on the old church of St-Raymond. During the expansive maritime period (15th – 17th centuries), ships from Audierne were away for much of the year, fishing cod off Newfoundland, whilst the export of dried fish, salt and grain also brought wealth to the town. Later development of technology put the emphasis on the conservation and manufacture of fish products. The Musée Maritime of Cap-Sizun (open mid June-September) is near the harbour. Inshore fishing of crab and lobster has always been important here – try the many restaurants with these specialities around the quays.

Audierne developed as a tourist resort from the coming of the railway at the end of 19th century, and it remains a popular leisure port. It has much to offer as a base of exploration: ferries to the île de Sein go from Ste-Evette, and a walk up the estuary to the lovely town of Pont-Croix is perfect for a relaxing day.

along behind beach • At fork, bear **R**, keeping close to beach of Trescadec • Pass another seaweed oven and bear **R** again soon after • Go in front of centre nautique, then down steps and ahead to road • There go **R**, opposite Chapelle de Ste-Evette • 200m turn **R** down steps onto beach (Or stay on the road, which the path rejoins not far ahead) • (**Little lighthouse among houses on opposite side of road**) **EITHER** follow road round to **L**, **OR** go to **R** (**toilets in little round building**) and walk in along the harbour wall

passerelle

37/2 Go **R** over passerelle, then **L** up towards road, turning **R** on footpath before it • At road, go ahead and follow up through pleasure port • **CA** right round harbour and across bridge over Goyen estuary • 175m turn **R** down lane by water (**NB development work here – follow local waymarking**) • Go round front of houses, down steps, and along beach • At end, go **R** on path round little headland • **CA** nearest water, to **R** of industrial buildings • Continue through P keeping close to edge, past memorial to those who have died at sea • Continue along beach, with church on hill above • Just beyond this, go **L** up steps, then bear **R** alongside wall • Follow path inland to little road • Turn **R** between two houses • Follow path **R** out to next headland

37/3 **Here is another seaweed oven and a series of WWII fortifications** • Follow path above rocky bays on low cliffs – easy walking • Descend to Plage de Kersiny • Turn **R** briefly on road, then **R** again on path above beach • At P, go across edge and continue on path • **CA** 2kms to headland of Ménez Drégan

10. PRACTICAL INFORMATION

SHOPS & SERVICES

- **Pointe du Raz** Maison du Site de la Pointe du Raz 02 98 70 67 18 www.pointeduraz.com Souvenir shops etc. and refreshments
- **Beuzec-Cap-Sizun** TO 02 98 70 55 51 www.beuzec-cap-sizun.fr Supermarket, butcher/delicatessen
- **Cléden-Cap-Sizun** www.cleden-cap-sizun.com
- **Plogoff** www.plogoff-pointeduraz.com
- **Primelin** Eco-marché supermarket on D784
- **Audierne** TO 02 98 70 12 20 www.audierne-tourisme.com All shops and services Mkt Sat am

ACCOMMODATION

Hotels

1. Hôtel de la Baie des Trepassés (on route) 29770 Plogoff 02 98 70 61 34 www.baiedestrepasses.com

Chambres d'hôte

2. M & Mme Conan (500m) Roz-Vein, 29770 Cléden-Cap-Sizun 02 98 70 31 32 http://pagesperso-orange.fr/roz-vein/ Open all year
3. Nicole Guezennec (600m) Kermeur, Pointe de Brézellec, 29770 Cléden-Cap-Sizun 02 98 70 .30 01 April – end September
4. Ar Ven Dero (750m) 29 rue des Hirondelles, Lescoff, 29770 Plogoff 02 98 70 38 24 Open all year
5. Mme Queinnec (on route) Villa Ker-Is, 29770 Audierne 02 98 70 20 28 www.villakeris.com June - September

Gîte d'étape/Camping

6. Camping-gîte de Loquéran (600m) 29770 Audierne 02 98 74 95 06 http://campgite.loqueran.free.fr Open all year

Camping

7. Camping Pors Peron (450m) 29790 Beuzec-Cap-Sizun 02 98 70 40 24 www.campingporsperon.com
8. Camping Municipal de Kermalero (1km) 29770 Primelin 02 98 74 84 75 March-October

TRANSPORT

Bus services: For buses on the peninsula, see www.viaoo29.fr

Taxi: Audierne Taxi 06 75 03 92 44

Boats to Sein, Molène and Ouessant: Penn ar Bed, Embarcadère de Sainte Evette, 29770 Audierne 02 98 70 70 70 www.pennarbed.fr

OTHER WALKS

10km circuit including the Pointe du Van and Baie des Trepassés

12km circuit, up and down the Goyen estuary between Audierne and Pont Croix.

For details see *Walking and other Activities in Finistere*

11. Ménez-Drégan - Le Guilvinec

Pays Bigouden: Baie d'Audierne
36 kms

This vast stretch of often wild, inhospitable and relatively uninhabited coastline ends in the conglomeration of villages around the Pointe de Penmarc'h, landmarked by lighthouses from different ages. It provides an undemanding walk of strong sensations, with Atlantic breakers pounding in to the accompaniment of strong and noisy winds. Much of the sandy beache is unsuitable for swimmers due to dangerous currents, but the Baie d'Audierne is a haven for water and sand-sports enthusiasts, especially around the Pointe de la Torche where the world wind surfing championship has been held.

This is largely a flat land where trees are scarce, but there is nevertheless much of environmental interest with important archaeological sites and a fragile ecological balance of tides, dunes and humid marshlands. Inland beyond the marshy lakes (étangs) with their vibrant bird-life, a surprising economic development of the 1960s has seen large areas of land under cultivation for the tulip industry by Dutch growers. To the south, fishing and marine transport (cabotage) have historically been the basis of the economy in small ports along the perilously rocky coast around Penmarc'h. Over the centuries prosperity and poverty, miraculous safety and tragic loss of life, salvage and wreckage have all come to the people of this low-lying area from the power and caprice of the tides.

SITE OF MÉNEZ DRÉGAN

The collapse of a cave revealed the existence of this remarkable site in the cliff-side. Excavations have yielded evidence of successive human occupation from c.450,000 - 300,000BC. Tools made from stone and animal bones were discovered, as well as hearths proving the early use of fire. An elephant's tooth was among the finds.

The Neolithic burial site on the headland of Souc'h directly above, including at least seven dolmens, is thought from its size and scale to have been a territorial boundary marker. Reconstruction work is underway here, and a future centre of interpretation is envisaged.

DIRECTIONS

38/1 **CA** on path round headland of Ménez Drégan, **skirting archaeological workings on cliffside where Palaeolithic remains were discovered** • **To see large Neolithic necropolis, take one of the paths to L up onto top here, then return to this point** • **CA** 600m • Just before lighthouse/firetower, go **L** up to alley-grave of Porz Poulhan, then return to coast path • **CA** to road and turn **R** around Porz Poulhan harbour (Bar/refreshments here and toilets in P̄)

ALLÉE COUVERTE DE PORZ POULHAN

This Neolithic burial monument was partly blown up in WWII. It has a paved funerary chamber, 10.8m long and 1.5-2m wide with over-lapping stone supports for greater stability. There were originally three roof stones, one of 15 tons. The site was used as a quarry in the Middle Ages. Finds include late Neolithic polished axes, silex arrowheads, round-bottomed pots and flat-bottomed vases. Bronze Age glass-beads were also discovered and Gallo-Romano funerary urns from the 2/3rd centuries.

♠ Plouhinec

D784

Neolithic necropolis

①

Porz Poulhan P 🏠

Ménez-Drégan

Palaeolithic site

D784

② ②

P

P P

Plozévet D2

②

Pors Poulhan

Map 38 N↑

⊢ 1km ⊣

The statue of a woman in traditional dress and coiffe ③
(headdress) marks the beginning of Pays Bigouden.

P P

③

🏠

①

P 🌿

P

④

🏠 Penhors ⛺ ⑤

Pouldreuzic (4kms)

D40

• **CA** past statue, follow road 400m, then turn **R** (by sign Rue de L'Océan) • Follow path above water and **CA** past picnic area **(where there is a seaweed oven – see p.79)**

38/2 At far end of P, go **R** down to beach • Follow beach 30m, then go **L** up sandy track (rock divides beach and track) • **CA** on road 130m, fork **R** on little road, follow to P with seaweed ovens • Turn off to **R** just before houses (through rocks), go a few metres across pebbles, then up steps • **CA** over plank bridge and tops of beaches • **(Caution** – after section of stone walling, look for danger sign where path has subsided ahead. Instead turn **L** here, then **R** 20m later. Follow this loop back to coast) • Track narrows again to footpath and goes onto beach • Bear **L**

157

MENHIR DES DROITS DE L'HOMME
(Menhir of the Rights of Man)

This large menhir is named after a French ship sunk by English frigates here in 1797. The *Droits de l'Homme* was part of a French fleet heading for Ireland when scattered by a storm. Its crew had already captured two English brigs and taken prisoners, including Major Pipon, a native of Jersey. He was on board when the ship went down but managed to escape death. In 1840 he returned here and had a memorial to the event engraved on the menhir by the shore. A painting (1853) of the battle by Léopold Le Guen is in the museum at Brest.

at once off beach and immediately **R** up steps • Keep ahead, bearing **R** to stay near beach • Go through ℗ (where road alongside bears 90° inland) and **CA** above beach in front of house wall • **CA** round edge of another large ℗ (Restaurant here too) • Menhir ahead by beach of Canté

The coast of the **BAY OF AUDIERNE** is a vast stretch of sandy beach separated from a humid marshy area of lakeland (étangs) by calciferous dunes and a high bank of pebbles. The marshes provide a haven for birds, and the ubiquitous reeds were used for thatching, as seen on local cottages, or animal bedding.

The dunes are under constant pressure from the sea and the impact of walkers, so it is important to keep to the paths and respect fencing arrangements. The Conservatoire du Littoral undertakes specific planting to anchor the natural defences against the powerful forces of the Atlantic Ocean. Plants such as sea-kale and marsh samphire, with their long roots, thrive among the pebbles and the salt-resistant marram-grass, which also expands its root system when covered by sand, creates a net-like structure of growth to help stabilise the dunes.

Musée de l'Amiral, Penhors

**38/3 From this point, a bank of pebbles above the beach
stretches ahead for many kms. CHOICE OF PATH: behind, along
the top (views to both sides) or on the beach. No need to leave
the beach for the next 15 kms •** *CA* 1.7 kms to Ⓟ by large lake • Go
between water and pebbles or on top of bank • 500m go through very
large Ⓟ and *CA* (**Another well-preserved seaweed oven to L of path**)
• *CA* to delightful small harbour of Penhors (**where there is a small
museum, Musée de l'Amiral, on littoral themes**) Refreshments
• Bear **R** along road • After 300m, off to L, is a fine chapel (usually
open) • *CA* on road or sand

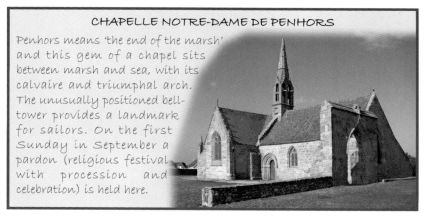

CHAPELLE NOTRE-DAME DE PENHORS

Penhors means 'the end of the marsh'
and this gem of a chapel sits
between marsh and sea, with its
calvaire and triumphal arch.
The unusually positioned bell-
tower provides a landmark
for sailors. On the first
Sunday in September a
pardon (religious festival
with procession and
celebration) is held here.

38/4 Where road turns inland, *CA* on sandy track • Crêperie • Where
path moves away from beach and crosses marsh to road, leave it and
continue along bank by beach • *CA* - either beach or pebbles or path
by lakes (**Try the sand for next few kms: despite the strong
breezes it is a magnificent beach and easy to walk on.**) • Pass Ⓟ
with stone house and seats • 300m after next Ⓟ and lifeguard station,
road inland is start of alternative route (GR34)

ALTERNATIVE ROUTE
·············· on MAP 39

An inland excursion from point 39/1 goes around a protected area of marshes and lakes, with a brief diversion by road to see the ruined chapel of Languidou

Chapelle de Languidou

This chapel dedicated to St-Kido (Guido) dates back to the early 15th century, with the stone tracery of a fine rose window remaining. When the chapel was semi-demolished in 1794 much of the stone was taken away for building projects elsewhere.

Etang de Kergalan

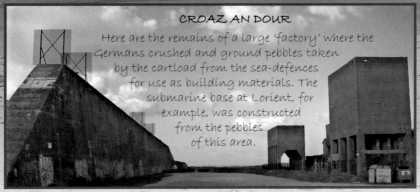

CROAZ AN DOUR

Here are the remains of a large 'factory' where the Germans crushed and ground pebbles taken by the cartload from the sea-defences for use as building materials. The submarine base at Lorient, for example, was constructed from the pebbles of this area.

160

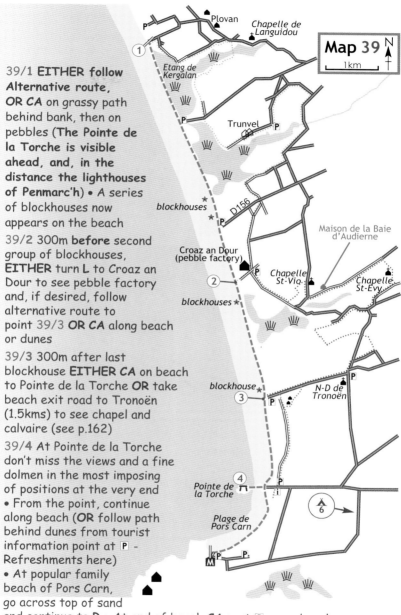

39/1 **EITHER** follow Alternative route, **OR CA** on grassy path behind bank, then on pebbles (**The Pointe de la Torche is visible ahead, and, in the distance the lighthouses of Penmarc'h**) • A series of blockhouses now appears on the beach

39/2 300m **before** second group of blockhouses, **EITHER** turn **L** to Croaz an Dour to see pebble factory and, if desired, follow alternative route to point 39/3 **OR CA** along beach or dunes

39/3 300m after last blockhouse **EITHER CA** on beach to Pointe de la Torche **OR** take beach exit road to Tronoën (1.5kms) to see chapel and calvaire (see p.162)

39/4 At Pointe de la Torche don't miss the views and a fine dolmen in the most imposing of positions at the very end • From the point, continue along beach (**OR** follow path behind dunes from tourist information point at P - Refreshments here) • At popular family beach of Pors Carn, go across top of sand and continue to **R** • At end of beach **CA** past P, over beach access track (**OR** cross road to visit archaeology museum - see p.162)

Map 39 N

1km

Plovan
Chapelle de Languidou
Etang de Kergalan
Trunvel
blockhouses
D156
Croaz an Dour (pebble factory)
Chapelle St-Vio
blockhouses
Maison de la Baie d'Audierne
Chapelle St-Evy
blockhouse
N-D de Tronoën
Pointe de la Torche
Plage de Pors Carn

ALTERNATIVE ROUTE ············· on MAP 39

From Craoz an Dour (near point 39/2) join a walking circuit taking in three chapels and the Maison de la Baie d'Audierne, and then rejoin the coast at point 39/3.

Outside the tiny **Chapelle de St-Vio** is the 'stone boat' in which the Irish saint is said to have reached this shore. There is also a small round Iron Age stele on a small mound nearby.

view from observation tower

At the **Maison de la Baie d'Audierne** there are exhibitions and environmental information, and organised events in the summer season. There is also a bird-watching tower here with excellent views over the lakes and to the coast.

The **Chapelle de St-Evy**, which dates from 1660, has an attractive setting in a pretty marshy valley.

On this route and also well worth a detour from the coast is the **Chapelle N-D de Tronoën**, the 'cathedral of the dunes' with its spire visible for miles around. It has one of the oldest (c1450) and most detailed calvaires in Brittany, with weathered figures still remarkably expressive.

N-D de Tronoën, calvaire

MUSÉE FINISTÉRIEN DE LA PRÉHISTOIRE

This excellent museum of Prehistory is just opposite the beach at Pors Carn. With both external displays and a large gallery area, it houses an extensive collection of artefacts from important sites all over Finistere, including local ones mentioned above. From Palaeolithic to Gallo-Roman periods, finds include examples of tools, weapons and pottery, as well as full burial reconstructions. Highly recommended.

PLAGE DE PORS CARN

This is a popular family beach with life-guard surveillance, refreshments and a children's playground. The area behind the beach is called Toull Gwin or 'Wine Hollow', recalling an 18th century event. A ship carrying wine from Bordeaux to England was driven ashore here and local people hurried to carry off and hide the dispersed barrels, or to drink as much as possible before the customs officers appeared.

ARCHAEOLOGY

The Pointe de la Torche with its striking location has known human occupation since at least Mesolithic times. A mass of shell-fish waste dating from this period (c10,000BC) and numerous flint tools were found by archaeologists. The remaining Neolithic dolmen and Bronze/Iron Age burial places now destroyed point to the continuity of usage of this 'headland of the hillock', as Beg an Dorchenn, its Breton name, signifies. (There are also WWII bunkers and emplacements on the point.) In the surrounding area, other excavations of significance revealed a Roman camp near Tronoën, where a statuette of the goddess Isis was found, and a necropolis at St-Urnel (or St-Saturnin) where numerous skeletons of early Bretons (5th-12th centuries) were excavated from a dark age settlement that vanished into the sand. The Musée de la Préhistoire (see previous page) has exhibits from these and many other sites.

Pointe de la Torche

40/1 At road, bear **R** to headland, then **L** past stone cross • **CA** past table of orientation and seaweed oven • At road bear **R**, then **R** at junction past another seaweed oven • 80m go **R** onto path • Continue in front of houses by sea • Join road at top of deep inlet, then bear **R** again by high wall • **From this point note the danger of high waves - to the right are the Rochers of St-Guénolé, with safety railings**

BLACK ROCKS OF ST-GUÉNOLÉ

The poet Chaucer, writing in the 14th century, makes this wild part of Brittany or Armoric the setting for the Franklin's Tale. Dorigen, wife of local knight Arveragus, fears for his safety on returning home by ship:

> But wolde God that all thise rokkes blake
> Were sunken into hell for his sake!
> Thise rokkes sleen myn heart for the feere.

These same black rocks claimed the lives of the Prefect of Finistere's family as they picnicked here in 1870, oblivious to the sudden potential for disaster lurking in the unpredictable waters. An iron cross set into the rock marks the spot. There has been loss of life in recent times here too, as warning signs note.

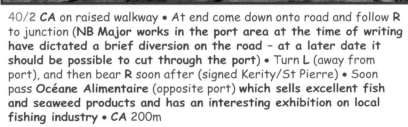

40/2 CA on raised walkway • At end come down onto road and follow **R** to junction (**NB Major works in the port area at the time of writing have dictated a brief diversion on the road – at a later date it should be possible to cut through the port**) • Turn **L** (away from port), and then bear **R** soon after (signed Kerity/St Pierre) • Soon pass **Océane Alimentaire** (opposite port) **which sells excellent fish and seaweed products and has an interesting exhibition on local fishing industry** • **CA** 200m

About 600m to the **L** here is the **TOUR CARRÉE** (1488), the remains of a 15th century church, with relief sculptures of ships.

• Turn **R** down narrow alley and bear **L** on footpath to join promenade behind sea wall • Follow this all the way to lighthouses visible ahead
CHAPELLE N-D DE LA JOIE This 15th century chapel (usually open) with maritime motifs was built in gratitude for safety from shipwrecks, and stands in a precarious position by the sea-wall.

- Bear **R** at end towards lighthouse and ahead through very narrow entrance on the wall • Then **L** across grassy area between ancient chapel and modern lighthouse to harbour of St-Pierre

PENMARC'H   The position of Penmarc'h and its surrounding villages made this an ideal staging post for north-south commercial routes, particularly the wine trade between Bordeaux and England. Local ships were also heavily involved in the movement of 'pastel de Toulouse' or the blue dye obtained from woad. The impressive scale of the church of St-Nonna (a 6th century arrival from Ireland) and the decorative ship motifs reflect the maritime prosperity of this area up to the 17th century.

THE LIGHTHOUSES

The earliest warning for sailors on this treacherous coast came from fires lit at the top of a tower (La Tour à Feu) beside the Chapelle St-Pierre, which dates back to the 15th century (and today houses exhibitions in summer). An oil-fuelled lamp was later employed before the tower was superseded as a lighthouse and found a new role as a semaphore base.

A functional lighthouse was built early in 1835, with its rapeseed oil lamp later replaced by a petrol one. Whereas similar buildings elsewhere were being adapted to electricity at the end of the century, it was decided to build a new lighthouse altogether at Penmarc'h.

The old structure now houses a maritime Centre of Discovery. Beside it, by the harbour, an early example of a lifeboat propelled by oars is on display.

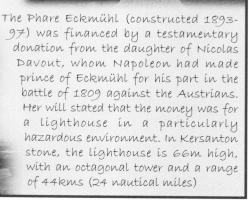

The Phare Eckmühl (constructed 1893-97) was financed by a testamentary donation from the daughter of Nicolas Davout, whom Napoleon had made prince of Eckmühl for his part in the battle of 1809 against the Austrians. Her will stated that the money was for a lighthouse in a particularly hazardous environment. In Kersanton stone, the lighthouse is 66m high, with an octagonal tower and a range of 44kms (24 nautical miles)

40/3 Walk around harbour and continue to **R** along coastal path behind sea wall • **CA** along road by shore • 800m, where road turns inland, go **ahead** on footpath above rocks (**Here there is a small memorial for those lost at sea**) • After 150m bear **L**, then **R** along road (**past base of old windmill**) • **CA** through parking past harbour of Kérity (Refreshments and provisions)

KÉRITY is an ancient community, the port of Penmarc'h since the 15th century. Houses from this period remain – take the rue de la Port to explore the narrow lanes – and the church of St-Thumette with its distinctive belfry near the harbour. The name is derived from 'charity', not the usual Breton 'ker' meaning 'settlement'. In summer a market is held at the port on Wednesdays.

• Past seaweed oven, **CA** along narrow path on dunes above beach, or

turn slightly inland to follow track behind beach and alongside marshy lakes

MENHIR DE LÉHAN In the marshy lakeland to the left stands this menhir of 4m. Its position reflects the changes in environment since the neolithic period, when the stone may have been placed to mark a source or stream.

• **Round headland, Le Guilvinec comes into view** • **CA** along magnificent beach, Plage du Ster, or on dunes, or behind on track • At end of beach, join wooden walkway, then **CA** along road to Men Meur

11. PRACTICAL INFORMATION

SHOPS & SERVICES

- **Tourisme Haut Bigouden** www.othpb.com
- **Penmarc'h** (which includes St-Guénolé, St-Pierre and Kerity)
  TO 02 98 58 81 44 www.penmarch.fr
- **Plozévet** (1.8kms) www.plozevet.fr

ACCOMMODATION

Hotels

1. Hotel Breiz Armor (on route) Penhors, 29710 Pouldreuzic
   02 98 51 52 53 www.breiz-armor.fr

Chambres d'hôte

2. Mme Trepos (1km) Kérongard-Divisquin, 29710 Plozévet
   02 98 54 31 09 http://monsite.wanadoo.fr/trepos
3. Mme Le Gars (100m) 30 rue du Romarin, 29760 St-Guénolé
   02 98 58 67 05 Open all year
4. Mme Le Pemp (50m) 55 Impasse Rulenn, Kerity 29760 02 98 58 65 69
   Open all year

Camping

5. Camping Le Littoral (400m) Penhors, 29710 Pouldreuzic
   02 98 54 35 44
6. Camping de la Torche (2km) Roz an Tremen, 29120 Plomeur
   02 98 58 62 82 www.campingdelatorche.fr
7. Camping de la Plage (on route) Ster Poulguen, 29760 Penmarc'h
   02 98 58 61 90 www.villagelaplage.com

TRANSPORT

Bus services: Buses connect the SW tip of Finistere with Quimper and
   Pont l'Abbé – see www.viaoo29.fr

Taxi: Maurice Autret 02 98 91 45 46 Plozévet
   Jacques Bouillet 02 98 58 55 56 Penmarc'h

OTHER WALKS

A 13km circuit of the Pointe de Penmarc'h includes the coastal route
given here and a connecting link from Kerity to Pors Carn via the marshy
hinterland (yellow balisage).

A really long (but fairly flat) circuit of 30kms starts from the Pointe de la
Torche and then explores the inland area around Plomeur (yellow
balisage).

12. Le Guilvinec-Benodet
Pays Bigouden: The Estuaries

40 kms

The easternmost part of Pays Bigouden sees a transition to calmer waters and a series of estuaries culminating in the serene beauty of the Odet. long sandy beaches dominate the actual littoral, whilst the inland stretches are mainly through light woodland.

This is a section of easy walking with varied scenery, and the option of taking short cuts via local foot-passenger ferries at certain times. It would be a shame, however, to miss out on historic Pont l'Abbé with its distinctively Breton atmosphere and excellent Musée Bigouden in the castle keep. The somewhat bland but famous seaside resort of Benodet, a mecca for holiday-makers and the yachting fraternity, contrasts with small ports like Lesconil, Loctudy, île Tudy and Ste-Marine which retain their character and simple appeal, particularly out of the main tourist season.

Crossing the Pont de Cornouaille provides a panorama of the Odet estuary around the Anse de Penfoul, down the coast to Benodet and Ste-Marine, its opposite neighbour, and out to the sea, where the îles Glenan are visible on the horizon on a clear day.

Men Meur

D53

Plobannalec

D102

Map 41 N

1km

D57

Le Guilvinec

①

Lesconil

Men
Meur

①

②

③

DIRECTIONS

41/1 Rejoin shore at Men Meur (with the eponymous huge rock - on private land)

Note the circular recesses in the flat rocks here. Cross bases or millstones were dug out in the 16-17th century, a time when many chapels and calvaires were put up. The large grained granite with almost horizontal fissures common along the coast here was most suitable for these purposes.

• **CA** along road 600m, then turn **R** into harbour of Le Guilvinec • Go ahead towards pier, then **L** along front of harbour buildings • **CA** through port, close to water • At end of port area follow footpath up

to road, turn **R** and go over bridge into Treffiagat • Bear **R** on walkway • **CA** on road at end of walkway • 40m bear **R** on footpath towards port (but not through it) • Follow road round to **L** • Stay on this road bearing **L** then **R** through houses (**OR** go on beach – various access points – if tide permits) • **CA** 300m to the Viviers des Lechiagat

41/2 Here turn **R** to dunes and bear **L** above excellent beach – (marshland and lake to left) • **CA** 3kms along beach (or on path behind • At bunker go briefly inland round little quarry and **CA** through Ⓟ • By some big boulders, cross track to beach, bearing **R** • Turn **L** to **CA** just behind dunes or go on beach • At end of beach, bear **R** through Ⓟ **(day marker by houses to left)** • Pass in front of house 100m in front of day mark **(there is a seasonal TO near the daymark)** • Continue round edge behind large rock formation and past stone cross

CROIX DES AMOUREUX

Traditionally this Lovers' Cross was a place for secret meetings and pledging fidelity. The original was vandalised in the 1920s and only fairly recently replaced on the authentic base.

• **CA** round little cove and towards more rock formations (There is also an old fishery on beach - see above - and seaweed oven by path)

41/3 At end of footpath **CA** up road • 100m at **TJ** go **R**, then bear **L** along coast around top of harbour, then bear **L** again • At road, go **L** (rue des Équipages)

LESCONIL is a small port, which, like Loctudy, developed late (19th century) as a centre of fishing. Langoustines is the speciality catch here, as a visit to the daily auction will reveal.

Follow road round top of port then bear **L** (do not continue into port) • 50m, after centre nautique, turn **R** down alley to beach, then **L** • Follow road or beach • Go along sand to top of harbour, then **R** on path along harbour wall and through houses straight ahead • 50m turn **R** • **CA** - road soon bends **L** then **R** • At shore go **L** • Turn **L** along narrow path above beach • Go ahead to causeway and turn **R** across it

This is **rue Eric Tabarly**, named after the famous French sailor lost at sea in 1998. He won one of the earliest trans-Atlantic races, sponsored by the Observer newspaper, in 1964 (receiving the Légion d'Honneur for this achievement) and again 1976.

• Turn **R** immediately at end of causeway • Follow path 200m to little road, then **R** along another causeway • Take **L** fork before beach • **CA** 900m on dunes above beach to far end

42/1 Follow path inland, down towards little road, then turn **R** down to beach again • Then **L** along path at top of beach • Keep ahead nearest to beach • Cross slipway and **CA** on path • Follow up onto little track and turn **R** • At large ℙ head straight up road • 300m turn **R** along rue Pen Arbut • **CA** 150m to **TJ** and turn **R** • 100m fork **R** on impasse de Prat an Asquel • At coast turn **L** • **CA** along beach 350m • At breakwater, go up slipway and turn **R** • 40m bear **R** along path back to shore • **CA** above beach on path 175m

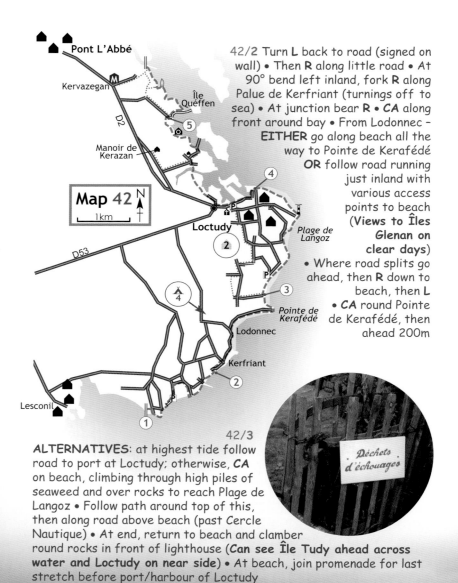

Map 42 N↑

Pont L'Abbé

Kervazegan

Île Quéffen

Manoir de Kerazan

1km

Loctudy

D2

D53

Plage de Langoz

Pointe de Kerafédé

Lodonnec

Kerfriant

Lesconil

42/2 Turn **L** back to road (signed on wall) • Then **R** along little road • At 90° bend left inland, fork **R** along Palue de Kerfriant (turnings off to sea) • At junction bear **R** • **CA** along front around bay • From Lodonnec – **EITHER** go along beach all the way to Pointe de Kerafédé **OR** follow road running just inland with various access points to beach (**Views to Îles Glenan on clear days**) • Where road splits go ahead, then **R** down to beach, then **L** • **CA** round Pointe de Kerafédé, then ahead 200m

42/3

ALTERNATIVES: at highest tide follow road to port at Loctudy; otherwise, **CA** on beach, climbing through high piles of seaweed and over rocks to reach Plage de Langoz • Follow path around top of this, then along road above beach (past Cercle Nautique) • At end, return to beach and clamber round rocks in front of lighthouse (**Can see Île Tudy ahead across water and Loctudy on near side**) • At beach, join promenade for last stretch before port/harbour of Loctudy

Déchets d'échouages

42/4 Join road at roundabout – main street to **L** for refreshments/provisions – otherwise go straight across and follow road round to **L** then to **R** (Can go right through harbour area if desired) • 350m cross to P on **L** and through it to visit church

Île Tudy

LOCTUDY

The origins of Loctudy (sacred place of Tudy) lay with the arrival of the saint from Britain in 5th century. An abbey later developed on the site he had chosen for his hermitage. The church of St-Tudy today has a magnificent Romanesque interior dating from the 11-12th centuries and merits a short detour.

Unusually, the port of Loctudy did not develop until the early 19th century, in what was essentially an agricultural area. The distinctive black and white Tourelle les Perdrix (partridge) marks the channel between Loc-Tudy and its neighbour Île-Tudy just across the water. A ferry runs between the two in season and the Vedettes de l'Odet also go from here to the Îles Glenan.

THE CHURCH OF ST-TUDY is the second priory on this spot, the earlier one having been destroyed by the Vikings around 915. The main part of the interior – nave, chancel and apse - dates from the late 11th century (12th century side-chapels) and the simple Romanesque vaulting is impressive. It is worth examining the columns, both top and bases, for their sometimes elaborate decoration. The name of the

little chapel beside the church, Porz-Bihan or 'small harbour' suggests that the sea once came right up to the precinct.

• Return to road and continue **L** along it • At roundabout turn **R** (rue du Kerilis) • **CA**, parallel with water as lane becomes footpath • Keep ahead at fork and ignore paths to left • Cross causeway, then up to road and follow **L** ahead

MANOIR DE KERAZAN (1.2kms) is an impressive 18th century château, once the home of Joseph Astor. The well-furnished rooms vividly recreate a sophisticated 19th century lifestyle, English billiard table included! There is also a fine collection of Quimper pottery – the full-sized cello is the largest musical instrument made from faïence in the world. The grounds include a farm (with produce) and a crêperie. (Open April-September)

• **DIVERSION**(1.2kms): take 1st **L**, follow to **TJ** and turn **R**, **CA** 500m to visit Manoir de Kerazan • **OTHERWISE**, continue to **R** of house at entrance to Dourdy Holiday Village (Signed Private road without issue) • Follow 350m to causeway to Île Garo but do not cross • Turn **L** along edge of creek (signed Quefflen 900m) between pine trees, skirting the holiday village • **CA** past old mill, through wooden barrier • Go round top of little creek, bearing **R** over slab bridge • Follow up flight of steps

42/5 **ALTERNATIVES: EITHER** Go **R** 300m to beginning of causeway and turn **L** along shore to menhir • **CA** past menhir and up into wood **OR**, if water is high, go **L** on road 400m, then bear **R** between rocks and immediately **R** or straight ahead (ends up in same place) to creek by menhir

> ### MENHIR DE PENGLAOUIC
> The siting of this menhir, which dates from c5000BC, gives an idea of the change in water levels over time. It marks the source of a stream feeding the river Pont l'Abbé, and also the boundary between the communes of Pont l'Abbé and Loctudy.

• At clearing in wood (where other path joins) go **ahead** (**observatory/hide to R here – vibrant bird life**) • An alternative path runs parallel on the shore • At junction of paths, go **R** past ruined house and jetty (**DIVERSION**: take path **L** here and **CA** on road to visit Maison du Pays Bigouden. Return same route)

MAISON DU PAYS BIGOUDEN The old Ferme de Kervazegan now houses an eco-museum (750m to the left here). Exhibitions and demonstrations provide an insight into rural life of the area over centuries. (Limited opening - consult TO 02 98 82 37 99)

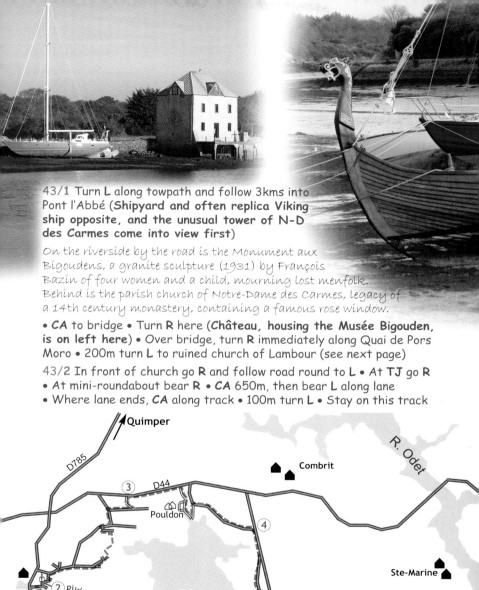

43/1 Turn **L** along towpath and follow 3kms into Pont l'Abbé (**Shipyard and often replica Viking ship opposite, and the unusual tower of N-D des Carmes come into view first**)

On the riverside by the road is the Monument aux Bigoudens, a granite sculpture (1931) by François Bazin of four women and a child, mourning lost menfolk. Behind is the parish church of Notre-Dame des Carmes, legacy of a 14th century monastery, containing a famous rose window.

• **CA** to bridge • Turn **R** here (**Château, housing the Musée Bigouden, is on left here**) • Over bridge, turn **R** immediately along Quai de Pors Moro • 200m turn **L** to ruined church of Lambour (see next page)

43/2 In front of church go **R** and follow road round to **L** • At **TJ** go **R** • At mini-roundabout bear **R** • **CA** 650m, then bear **L** along lane • Where lane ends, **CA** along track • 100m turn **L** • Stay on this track

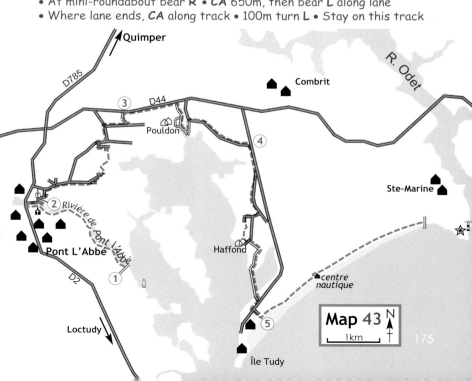

Quimper

D785

Combrit

R. Odet

③ D44

Pouldon

④

Ste-Marine

② Rivière de Pont L'Abbé

Pont L'Abbé

Haffond

D2

centre nautique

①

Loctudy

⑤

Île Tudy

Map 43 N

1km

PONT L'ABBÉ

The name of the town reflects the original bridging of the river by monks of Loctudy. The earliest château on this spot was built in the 11th century and it was the stronghold of the Barons du Pont in subsequent centuries. Nothing remains today of the extensive ramparts, deep moat and two drawbridges, but the Keep that now stands shorn of its fortifications is still very impressive. Since 1955 it has housed the excellent Musée Bigouden, which amongst many other things of interest includes a fine collection of traditional local furniture, costumes and coiffes (the tall lace headdresses of the region).

There was much support in this area for the revolt of 1675 against new taxes, including the infamous papier timbre levy (for paper used in all legal transactions), although in rural areas the main grievance was against the autocratic behaviour of land-owners. The château was pillaged and burnt at this time, and monks were made to sign the 'Code Breton' to avoid damage to the monastery des Carmes.

Pont l'Abbé was a busy port in the 18th and 19th centuries, with the export of grain, fish, potatoes and wood. Houses from this period of prosperity remain in many streets of the town, as well as older examples in the little lanes. In July the town hosts the Fête des Brodeuses, a flamboyant festival of Breton dancing, music and colourful costumes.

between fields • At road, go ahead 80m to **TJ** and turn **L** • 200m at **TJ** go **R** • 150m turn **L** • 250m at mini-roundabout go **R** • **CA** on this quiet country road 400m, then turn **L** down track into trees • Keep ahead downhill to main road (D44)

43/3 Turn **R** and walk alongside road for nearly 1km • Turn **R** down

EGLISE DE LAMBOUR

This ruined chapel, in part dating back to the 13th century, remains, in its towerless state a symbolic reminder of the 1675 revolt of the 'Red Bonnets'. Much supported in this area, the uprising against harsh new taxation and an oppressive aristocracy led to savage reprisals, including the destruction of towers of churches whose bells had summoned support for the rebellion. Fine stone carvings remain.

track signed to Pouldon • Follow this lane to estuary • **CA** on same track, which then turns uphill and away from water • Ignore all paths off • At road go **R** and stay on it 1.2km to junction

43/4 Here go **R** along the wide verge beside the main road • At next junction turn **R** • Follow this quiet road 750m, then turn **R**, signed Le Haffond • 150m go straight ahead past bins • 50m go **R** at fork • Follow this lane, soon bearing **L** • **CA** on track to hamlet • At road turn **L**, then immediately **R** on rough track • Follow track to water • Turn **L** along the sillon (**a narrow road across the estuary with views ahead to Île Tudy and across the water to Loctudy**) • Go

Île Tudy

ahead to main road and turn **R** • 100m take first road on **L** (rue des chardons bleus) • At end **EITHER** go ahead across 🅿 and grass to water's edge **OR** go **R** to see the little port of Île Tudy, connected by ferry to Loctudy in season

43/5 Turn **L** along coast (beach or grassy track, then path above)
From here there are views out to the îles Glenan on the horizon - the tower of fort on île Cigogne is a landmark.

• **CA** behind beach to *centre nautique* where path turns inland behind it • Then **EITHER CA** on path behind dunes for 1.5kms **OR** go back onto beach to walk along the sand past a bunker

Terns' nests

44/1 At end of beach, CA along sandy path out to Pointe de Combrit **(where there is an old stone customs house)** • **CA** through Ⓟ and along road 100m Just to the left here is the Fort de Ste-Marine (1862) of Napoleon III, now used as an arts centre. It has a 'twin' across the water in Benodet.

• Turn **R** down footpath, past lighthouse, then follow **L** along Odet estuary • **CA** across end of road and skirt public park, then follow **L** inland • 200m, turn **R** past metal barrier, then **R** again at next one • At **TJ** turn **L** • At next **TJ** turn **R** on

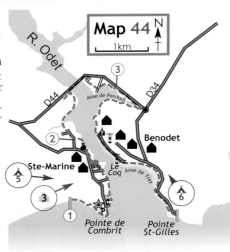

STE-MARINE

This charming and unspoilt little port by the mouth of the Odet was for many years the home of Jacques de Thézac, a philanthropist who created the Abris du Marins – shelters for impoverished fishermen and sardine-workers. One example remains here on the quay which is named after him. (At the time of writing it is being renovated as a centre of interpretation for his work.) The waterside is now dominated by cafés and restaurants alongside the picturesque 16th century chapel of Ste-Marine.

Café de la Cale

Pont de Cornouaille, constructed in 1970-2

main road • **CA** 400m to Chapelle de Ste-Marine, down steps to harbour and bear **L** (restaurants) • Bear **R** along harbour wall to Café de la Cale • Immediately beyond it, go **L** up steps and **ahead** to end of road

44/2 Turn **R** and **CA** 200m • At fork go **R** • **CA** 1km on path near water, crossing creek and stream and bearing **R** in open area • At P under Pont de Cornouaille, **CA** to next P then double back under bridge and bear **R** up staircase on south side of bridge • At top, walk over bridge (**great views of the Odet estuary and the town of Benodet**) • At other end of bridge, go **R** down steps onto track and turn **R** downhill away from main road • Take first path on **L**, past barrier into wood and **L** at cross-paths soon after • **CA** 300m to track, cross (slightly **L**) and **CA** on narrow winding path above water

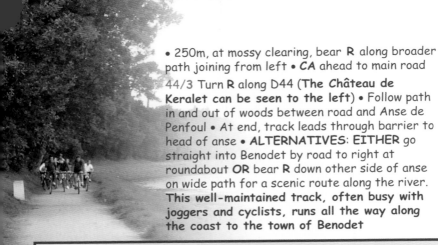

• 250m, at mossy clearing, bear **R** along broader path joining from left • **CA** ahead to main road

44/3 Turn **R** along D44 (**The Château de Keralet can be seen to the left**) • Follow path in and out of woods between road and Anse de Penfoul • At end, track leads through barrier to head of anse • **ALTERNATIVES: EITHER** go straight into Benodet by road to right at roundabout **OR** bear **R** down other side of anse on wide path for a scenic route along the river. **This well-maintained track, often busy with joggers and cyclists, runs all the way along the coast to the town of Benodet**

BENODET

The name of Benodet reflects its impressive position at the mouth of the Odet river. Today the town is dominated by expensive boats, gracious villas, smart shops and exceptionally ugly modern architecture, a place where the smell of money vies with that special scent of an estuary nearing the sea. Beyond the marina there are sandy beaches on each side of the Phare du Coq, the little lighthouse named after an oddly shaped rock. The taller Phare de la Pyramide, just inland, is so called because it replaced an earlier wooden structure of that shape. Across the water Benodet's pretty neighbour Ste-Marine was connected by chain ferry until as recently as 1972, when the Pont de Cornouaille was built. Leisure ferries now run from the harbour out to the îles Glenan, Loctudy or up river to Quimper.

A feat of the imagination can conjure up the simpler appeal of an earlier Benodet grouped around the little church of St-Thomas Beckett on the sea-front in this superb natural environment. Originally a commercial port, the blossoming of tourism in the late 19th and early 20th centuries saw the development of a spa town and pleasure port, playground particularly of rich Parisians and English. This influx of wealth inevitably brought physical and atmospheric change to the character of the town. Benodet was also a magnet for writers and artists in this period. Emile Zola was staying near here when he conceived Germinal, his dark novel of a miners' strike, after talking with Alfred Giard, the deputy of Valenciennes, who was well-versed in the working conditions in northern France.

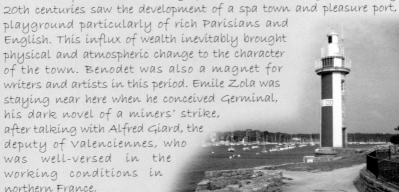

At the marina, where there are refreshments, the path continues along front by the harbour and the quay from which ferries leave for the Îles Glenan. The mouth of the estuary and islands beyond are visible.

EGLISE ST-THOMAS This church was founded in the 13th century and retains the choir section from this early period as well as a 15th century north chapel. It is dedicated to Thomas à Beckett who was murdered in Canterbury cathedral in 1170 on the orders of Henry II.

• Follow road above beach to little lighthouse (**the town centre is to the L here, for shops and services**)

THE PHARE DU COQ was built in 1848, then rebuilt in 1947 after destruction by the German occupation. Just off to the left here is the Fort du Coq (1862), parallel to that of Ste-Marine. It is now used by the sailing school.

• **CA** along lengthy sands of Anse de Trez • From there, go on by road down to Pointe St-Gilles

Fort du Coq

the final stretch...

12. PRACTICAL INFORMATION

SHOPS & SERVICES
- **Le Guilvinec** TO 02 98 58 29 29 www.leguilvinec.com Mkt Tue am
- **Loctudy** TO 02 98 87 53 78 www.loctudy.fr Mkt Tue am
- **Pont l'Abbé** TO 02 98 82 37 99 www.pontlabbe-lesconil.com Mkt Thurs
- **Combrit-Ste-Marine** TO 02 98 56 48 41 www.ville-de-combrit.fr
- **Benodet** TO 02 98 57 00 14 www.benodet.fr Mkt Mon am

ACCOMMODATION
Chambres d'hôte
1. Mme Kerveillant (350m) 02 98 58 90 48. 9 rue Jean Jaures, 29730 Le Guilvinec Open all year
2. M.Hervé Belbeoc'h (500m) Ferme de Poulpeye, rue de Kerpaul, 29750 Loctudy 02 98 87 94 38 www.poulpeye.pursud.org
3. Mme Monique Phuez (400m) 36 rue André Chevrillon, 29120 Ste-Marine 02 98 56 30 20 Open all year

Camping
4. Camping les Hortensias (600m) 38 rue des tulipes, 29750 Loctudy 02 98 87 46 64 www.leshortensias.chez-alice.fr
5. Camping le Helles (500m) 55 rue du Petit Bourg, Ste-Marine, 29120 Combrit 02 98 56 31 46 www.le-helles.com
6. Camping du Poulquer (200m) 23 rue du Poulquer, 29950 Benodet 02 98 57 04 19 www.campingdupoulquer.com

TRANSPORT
Bus services: via Quimper   www.viaoo29.fr

Taxi: Taxi Guilvinistes 02 98 58 93 93   Le Guilvinec
André Jany 02 98 87 31 89 Pont L'Abbé
Taxi Bénodétois 02 98 57 28 00 Benodet

Ferry: (foot-passengers only) connects Loctudy and Île-Tudy
Vedettes de l'Odet from Benodet to Îles Glenan –
www.vedettes-odet.com

OTHER WALKS
Circuit of 7kms starting from parking near the Menhir de Léhan, with another menhir and the Chapelle St-Fiacre on the route.

From the parking area with information point just west of the Pont de Cornouaille, follow a 9km circuit (yellow balisage) up the river Odet and round the shore to Combrit before returning through the Bois de Roscouré.

GLOSSARY

aber - estuary
algue - seaweed
allée couverte - neolithic grave
anse - bay, creek
auberge - inn
auberge de jeunesse - youth hostel
baie - bay
balade - a walk
balisage - waymarking
bourg - large village
calvaire - calvary
centre nautique -
    sailing/watersports centre
chambres d'hôte - B&B
chemin - small road, track, path
chemin creux - sunken track
commune - local administrative
    area/parish
Corps de Garde - guardhouse
corsair - licensed pirate
côte - coast
daymark - (see seamark)
dépot pain - point of sale for bread
digue - dike, bank
dolmen - neolithic/bronze age
    burial chamber
embarcadère - landing stage
enez - island
éperon barrée - fortified spur
épicerie - grocery
étang - lake
fontaine - spring/fountain
four - oven
gîte d'étape - basic overnight
    accommodation
goémon - seaweed

grève - shore
halles - covered market
île - island
îlot - island, small island
La Poste - Post Office
lavoir - washing place
mairie - town hall
maison de retraite -
    old peoples' home
manoir - manor
menhir - standing stone
moulin - mill
musée - museum
naufrage - shipwreck
oppidum - iron age settlement
passerelle - footbridge
pays - local area, country
phare - lighthouse
plage - beach
port de plaisance - marina
presse (maison de la) - newsagent
quai - quay
rando-gîte/rando-plume -
    basic overnight
    accommodation specifically
    for walkers
relais - inn, staging post
rocher - rock
route - road
rue - street
seamark - navigation aid visible in
    daylight
sentier piéton - pedestrian
    footpath
sillon - spit of land/sandbank
vedette - passenger boat/ferry
vivier - fish tank

PLANNING

This type of walking (over a distance) works best with a degree of planning, from consulting tide times or the weather forecast to organising transport for the return leg of a linear route. Some stretches of the coast are well-served with refreshment facilities and accommodation in the summer season, but completely shuttered and deserted at other times of year. Some estuaries have ferry services in the summer season which will save time and energy, and many coastal areas have good bus services when demand is high at this time. The French series of blue IGN maps (see www.ign.fr) may also be useful for giving a wider view of the area.

Tides

One essential factor for walkers to consider is the tides: there are two high tides and two low tides each 24 hours, but the actual times of these change gradually from day to day. Sometimes it will be possible to walk across bays at low tide and save a considerable distance, but safety should be a prime consideration. It is a sensible basic measure to buy a tide-timetable from a newsagent or tourist office according to your chosen location. Be especially careful not to get cut off when crossing causeways to islands.

Seasons

Walking the coast is sensational at any time of year – and many of my most enjoyable days have been in winter months – but generally I would recommend May/June or September/October. At these times the weather should not be too hot or cold and the paths will be relatively deserted. Remember that the water will be warmer in the later part of the year if you plan to include a lot of swimming.

If on the other hand you prefer crowds and like walking in blazing sunshine, then try July or August – the main advantage of this holiday period is that everything will be open, but accommodation will be harder to find on spec. 'Honey-pot' tourist locations– such as the Pointe du Raz - attract visitors all year round but otherwise the walking paths are rarely busy. Beaches are so huge and so numerous that even in high season finding one's own space is never a problem in Finistere.

Transport

For a day's outing, thinking about the return journey in advance is a sensible precaution. The options are either to set out for a day's walk and get public transport or a lift back from the finish point, or – and this is my preferred method – drive/cycle to the end point first thing, get a bus or taxi to the chosen start point and then walk all day to reach your own transport. This means the time taken for the walk can be more flexible.

It is surprisingly easy to find a bus in some coastal areas, whilst they are non-existent in others. Tourist offices will provide timetables for their entire area and help you through the myriad of qualifying clauses and inter-connections. Bus timetables are very reliable – often to the minute, so be at the stop on time!

Taxis are a more expensive, but generally reliable option. Local taxi phone numbers are given at the end of each section in the text. (Pre-booking is possible online – see www.taxi-finistere.com) It is better to arrange this for the morning from the 'finish' point and then walk towards where your car/bike is parked, as the timing of walks is hard to predict accurately, and you will have more option of lingering.

Trains connect the major cities and some smaller towns, but the coast itself is not well-served by train. It would be possible to walk from Morlaix to Brest and then return from there by train. Routes and timetables can be consulted on www.voyages-sncf.com. For bus services in Finistere, consult www.viaoo29.fr

Accommodation

Taking several days or even weeks over a coastal walk really does need some thought about accommodation, and much will depend on what time of year you choose. There is a variety of possibilities to take into consideration: camping sites (not only for those with tents – see below), rando-gîtes/rando-plumes (walkers' hostels), B&Bs and hotels are the main categories.

Camp-sites along the coast are numerous, but opening times vary enormously from July and August only, to all year round. It is well worth noting that many will hire a caravan or a berth in a chalet to those without tents in search of an overnight stay. Checking this out in advance, however, is important as any accommodation well-placed for the coastal path is often fully booked up weeks ahead.

The same is true of B&Bs and hotels near the sea. Tourist offices may be able to help with rooms to let in private houses in high season when other options are fully booked.

The reverse problem is that off season – a much better time to walk in my opinion - choices of accommodation on the coast are limited and in

some areas non-existent. There is always somewhere available further afield, but don't underestimate those extra kilometres to an inland location at the end of a long day's walking in a fresh sea breeze.

Some suggestions for accommodation are given at the end of each section, but there are many more options. Contact details for the local tourist offices are provided too – often their websites give details of a range of accommodation.

The Brittany Walks website (www.brittanywalks.com) is building an accommodation list which may be useful for coastal walking.

Provisions

Some thought should be given to basic provisions if you are walking a section of the coast without large settlements. Small villages and hamlets may have a bar where a bottle of water could be purchased, but it is safer to be equipped in advance. A 1.5 litre bottle is the sensible minimum for a day's walk – on a hot day, twice as much may be needed.

Try to take basic food requirements at all times as shops/crêperies/restaurants at a suitable stopping point may be closed. Sandwiches, fruit and chocolate are the staples, or a pasta/rice salad is a good idea if you have facilities for preparation.

My common daily ration is one or two hard-boiled eggs, an orange and a container of dried fruit and nuts, to be supplemented by a loaf of good bread from a bakery before setting off (and often a pain aux raisins for that mid-morning break). The important point, as I have discovered, is not to be absolutely dependent on finding a shop open at the right time or place.

Equipment

Basic Water
Emergency food – e.g. chocolate!
Proper walking shoes/boots
Wet-weather gear – minimum a plastic poncho
Whistle
Mobile phone
Hat (with strap)
Sun-cream (the sea-breeze is deceptive – protection is essential)
Map/guidebook

Extras Stick/poles
Binoculars
Camera
Compass/GPS unit

Emergency Telephone numbers

From ANY mobile phone call **112** (to be passed on to a specific service)
Otherwise: **18** Pompiers (fire, accident, medical help)
15 SAMU (medical emergency in urban location)
17 Police

RECOMMENDED ROUTES

* easy   ** moderate   *** strenuous

LESS THAN A DAY (STROLLS)
Roscoff ferry port to town centre*
Around Meneham*
Around Pointe de Penhir (staying on level paths)*
Plomarc'h (Douarnenez)* TOP CHOICE
Around Pointe du Van (staying on level paths)*
Around the Pointe du Raz (staying on level paths)*
From Pont l'Abbé down the estuary to Menhir de Penglaouic*
Anse de Penfoul to Benodet*

ONE DAY (*Out and back*)
Portsall to Argenton/Porspoder*
Le Conquet to St-Mathieu** TOP CHOICE
Camaret to Kerloc'h**
Penmarc'h to Guilvinec*
Loctudy to Pont l'Abbé*

ONE DAY (*Linear*)
From Moguériec to Bay of Kernic**
Around Beg Monom* (north of Plouguerneau)
Aber Benoit south side**
Portsall to Lanildut**
St Mathieu to Brest**/*** TOP CHOICE EQUAL
Pont de Térénez to Landévennec/Le Loc'h**
Camaret to Lostmarc'h*** TOP CHOICE EQUAL
Douarnenez to Pointe du Millier***

TWO TO THREE DAYS
Portsall to Brest**
Camaret to Morgat*** TOP CHOICE
Douarnenez to Audierne***
Audierne to Le Guilvinec*

A WEEK
Portsall to Morgat*/***
Douarnenez to Benodet*/***

187

INDEX of PLACES

A listing of the main places mentioned, and better known headlands and beaches (main reference is bolded)

Other books by Wendy Mewes

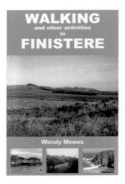

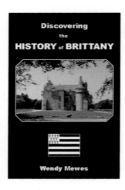

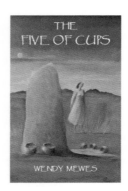

www.wendymewes.net

BRITTANY WALKS ASSOCIATION

Brittany Walks is an association based in Finistere with the aim of promoting and developing walking and historical interest in Brittany through the medium of the English language.

The association organises events, including regular guided walks and outings, talks, courses and workshops in English. It also works with tourist organisations and other associations to help English speakers, of whatever nationality, to explore and discover the history and landscape of Brittany.

In addition, Brittany Walks provides an internet-based information service.

For details of the association, membership and events:

www.brittanywalks.com

WALKING THE
BRITTANY
COAST

VOL 1: MONT ST-MICHEL TO MORLAIX
JUDY SMITH

www.reddogbooks.com

Vol 2 back cover photos:
near Enez Coun; Château de Taureau; Bay of Douarnenez; Port of Douarnenez